Holding
Audience
Attention

**How to Speak
with Confidence,
Substance
and Power**

L. Perry Wilbur

PICCADILLY BOOKS, LTD
COLORADO SPRINGS, COLORADO

Cover design by Michael Donahue

Piccadilly Books, Ltd.
P.O. Box 25203
Colorado Springs, CO 80936, USA

International sales and inquires contact:
Empire Publishing Service
20 Park Drive
Romford Essex RM1 4LH, UK
or
Empire Publishing Service
P.O. Box 1344
Studio City, CA 91614, USA

Library of Congress Cataloging-in-Publication Data

Wilbur, L. Perry.
    Holding audience attention: how to speak with confidence, substance, and power / L. Perry Wilbur.
        p. cm.
    Includes index.
    ISBN 0-941599-50-7
    1. Public speaking. I. Title.
PN4121.W3838 2000
808.5'1--dc21   99-462159

Simultaneously Published in Australia, UK, and USA
Printed in Canada

DEDICATION

This book is dedicated to three great public speaking professors back in my college days at Memphis State University. Brad White, Eugene Bence, and Don Streeter first inspired me as a speaker and showed me the great potential of communication.

Ray Mofield was a great friend and inspiration to me during my graduate studies in Communications at Murray State University in Murray, Kentucky.

I also want to thank John Hunt for his friendship and all his help in my work as an instructor of Public Speaking for the United States Navy and also at Florida Community College at Jacksonville.

It is a great adventure to stand before an audience and do your best to inform, inspire, entertain, or persuade them. My sincere thanks to all the audiences I have spoken to, for their feedback, and the inspiration they gave me.

CONTENTS

PART
I

SKILL IN SPEAKING
IS POWER

1

THE ABILITY TO SPEAK WELL IS POWER

Ever stop to realize just how important speaking ability is in your life? What if someone waved a wand and you found yourself unable to utter any more words or sentences? Your life would come to a silent halt.

The truth is, skill in speaking is power. It can bring you success, money, prestige, more satisfaction, and much greater achievement during your life, plus plain fun of being a communicator.

The spoken word helps keep this old planet turning. Once you learn how to develop various kinds of speeches and to present them with confidence and effectiveness, the world must take note of you.

Sigmund Freud summed up the great power of words very effectively: "Words have a magical power. They can bring either the greatest happiness or deepest despair; can transfer knowledge from teacher to student; words enable the orator to sway his audience and dictate its decisions. Words are capable of arousing the strongest emotions and prompting all men's actions."

A YOUNG PRESIDENT DESCRIBES
THE NEW FRONTIER
Flashback to January 20, 1961. Inauguration Day was a cold, snowy one in Washington. On the inaugural platform sat Dwight Eisenhower, who had been America's oldest president. Beside him was John Kennedy, who at 43 was the youngest elected president.

A good idea of the hope, resolve, and vigor of John Kennedy was expressed in a particularly memorable statement from the inaugural address: "Let every nation know, whether it wishes us well or ill, that we shall pay any price, bear any burden meet any hardship, support any friend, oppose any foe to assure the survival and the success of liberty."

It was almost at the end of his speech that Kennedy spoke one of the most famous and often quoted lines of his career; "Ask not what your country can do for you; ask what you can do for your country." Millions have long remembered him speaking these lines, with his hand jabbing the air to strengthen what he said. The lines, along with others, are carved in stone at Kennedy's grave site in Arlington National Cemetery. Kennedy obviously believed in a strong sense of loyalty and personal willingness to roll up one's sleeves and go to work for America. His famous quote reached many young people and sparked a greater feeling of patriotism in them.

WILLIAM JENNINGS BRYAN
KNEW THE POWER OF THE SPOKEN WORD
William Jennings Bryan was a very popular speaker for some 25 years. His most famous address was the "Cross of Gold" speech, which he delivered before the Democratic convention at Chicago on July 8, 1896. There were 20,000 people present.

Bryan had a strong talent for immediately grabbing an audience's attention and holding it throughout his speech. His voice, the way in which he led the audience, and his dramatic appeals all combined to make him a dynamic speaker. Here is the introduction of his "Cross of Gold" speech:

> I would be presumptuous, indeed, to present myself against the distinguished gentlemen to whom you have listened if this were a mere measuring of abilities; but this is not a contest between persons. The humblest citizen in all the land, when clad in the armor of a righteous cause, is stronger than all the hosts of error. I come to speak to you in defense of a cause as holy as the cause of liberty—the cause of humanity.

Developing skill in speaking can bring more power to the following areas of your life:

1. Becoming a better speaker brings power in your school or college life.

2. Speech ability brings power in landing a job or career and getting ahead in it.

3. Speaking effectiveness brings more power in business.

4. Speaking skill adds to your power in the professions.

5. Speech ability brings more power in your personal life.

POWER IN YOUR SCHOOL OR COLLEGE LIFE

Speaking ability helps to overcome shyness. It's like swimming; the more you do the better you become. I remember a girl in the high school speech class I taught in Louisiana. She was very shy at first, but halfway through the school term she seemed to find herself and her personality. Her speeches in class improved remarkably. Her parents were very pleased with her development.

In my own case, speech training opened up an entire new world for me. One plus was the fact that it made me realize that there are good ideas for speeches everywhere. I had first taken speech in high school and liked it, so I made it my major subject in college.

The Speech department of my college, Memphis State University (now The University of Memphis), invited me to take part in the filming of a color documentary about the historic Shiloh battlefield some hundred miles east of Memphis.

I was one of ten actors in the film called "Shiloh: Portrait of a Battlefield." The fields there are silent now, but after several days on location at the national park, the solemn atmosphere of the place got to me.

I listened in the evening breeze and could almost hear the sound of distant gunfire and booming cannons. Acting as an aide to General Grant in one scene, I walked the River Road beside him as he planned his strategy.

I saw trenches everywhere, listing the names of Union and Confederate states and the losses on each side. The cannons, sitting silently in the fields, became etched in my mind.

As a confederate officer in a campfire scene, I huddled over a map, convinced throughout the scene that one of the restless horses beside us was going to kick me or all of the actors.

To this day, this award-winning film is shown several times a day at the historic Shiloh National Park lodge.

My experience at Shiloh gave me some excellent material for a speech about the battlefield and what it was like to be in a film about the place. It also led me to write both an article and song about Shiloh. The article was published, and my song was later recorded and nationally released.

POWER IN BUSINESS AND THE PROFESSIONS

In the words of Clarence Randall, former Chairman of the Board of Inland Steel Corporation, "We are cut off from the public because we can neither write nor speak the English language with clarity and force." It seems clear that if a person can learn to be a stronger communicator, his or her business, or professional career, is bound to be more successful.

Gabriel Heatter was one of the Mutual Broadcasting System's most profitable and best known newscasters. He kept huge wartime audiences glued to their radio sets during the dark days of World War II. His deep baritone voice and famous attractive opening line were unmistakable: "Ah, there's good news tonight."

Heatter rose from the slums of New York to earn $400,000 a year. This was an enormous amount for those years. His initial reputation was made the night he melodramatically ad libbed, for 45 minutes without a pause, the New Jersey state prison electrocution of Bruno Hauptmann—the kidnapper/murderer of the Charles Lindbergh child.

Heatter's marathon coverage of the execution drew more than 50,000 letters from listeners, stirring countless millions across America. This broadcast lifted him from the ranks of minor newsmen and turned him into a $3500 a week commentator. And that, too, was a fortune in those days.

Heatter developed the ability to pack a lot of information into his newscasts. He was very factual, but sometimes used semi-editorial interpolations in his reports. He would often broadcast from an unusual place, such as a coal mine or an airplane. These techniques helped to make him unique. He is well-worth noting here, because he shows what can happen when you spot an opportunity and make the most of it. He was in the right place at the right time, but his style and unusual voice were what put him over, along with his marathon coverage of the electrocution.

Billy Graham has earned his place near the top of any list of dynamic communicators of the century. He has been criticized for playing on the emotions of his audiences, yet there is no doubt that his compelling voice, style of delivery, variety of material, and excellent gestures combine to reach the majority of every large group that hears him speak. His speaking ability has made him the best known evangelist of the century.

More typical examples of people interested in improving their job or standing in the community—via speaking ability—include athletes, plumbers, doctors, salesmen, and secretaries. Even homemakers can benefit from better speaking skills. More skill with the spoken word can improve a plumber's business relations with customers. Such plumbers can take a more active part in plumber associations.

Doctors who can speak effectively are sometimes invited to speak before annual meetings of the American Medical Association. They are also invited to address local, state, and regional medical organizations. As a medical authority, a doctor makes a fine guest speaker before various groups, and such appearances do much to make doctors well known.

Skill as a speaker can open up new club memberships for homemakers. A homemaker may wish to organize a special group of friends or neighbors herself. Confidence as a public speaker thus increases the enjoyment for a homemaker and enables her to pursue more social, civic, charitable, and business, or political interests.

Ability in speaking can also pay off well when attending a business conference or convention. A great many business people take a visible part in the on-going work and advancement of their cities and surrounding areas. They raise funds, do charity work, promote worthy causes, stimulate youth interests, and sponsor a variety of meetings themselves. Better use of the spoken word is bound to help them and add to their reputations in the business community.

Keep in mind also that people in the business world are sometimes asked by their superiors to present a report, speak to a department, section, or branch of the company, or sell the features of some new proposal or venture. Being able to plan an effective oral presentation and deliver it is a definite stepping-stone to advancement in your business field.

SPEAKING CAN STIR THE EMOTIONS

Remember actor Paul Newman in the classic film about a chain gang of convicts? The title was "Cool Hand Luke." The cruel warden frequently voiced the same statement when harsh punishment was in order. When Luke mimicked the warden one day, he was lashed with a whip, which knocked him down a hillside. True to his character, the warden sounded off with the line he liked: "What we've got here is a failure to communicate."

Luke refused to knuckle under and submit to the harsh treatment, so in the warden's view he was not getting the message. Prison is not supposed to be easy, but the chain gang concept of earlier times went too far in its treatment of convicts.

Proof that speaking can and does arouse the emotions can be seen in the impact of past and modern speakers. Take Adolph Hitler, for example. Millions believe Hitler was one of the forerunners of the Antichrist. He had a gift for speaking and stirring the emotions of large audiences, but, unfortunately, he used his considerable speaking ability for evil.

Hitler became an expert at knowing just how to build emotion in a crowd and how to hold each crowd in the palm of his hand. The crowds he spoke to in the late 1930s, and later, became as mere clay in his hands. This was, to a large degree, the source of his power. As a stage manager and mob psychologist, Hitler was able to whip each crowd into such a frenzy that the crowd became one single unit that he could mold and use as he wished.

HOW HITLER CONTROLLED THE EMOTIONS

How did Hitler accomplish this power over the people? He did it by gaining control over the emotions of the audience.

Hitler always let a large crowd in a hall wait for an hour or two before he arrived to speak. He never arrived on the scene until he was certain that the crowd waiting for him was keyed up with anticipation and tenseness. It was all standard routine for Hitler. He had the walls of the halls where he spoke covered with Nazi slogans. Marching and other military music was played by bands, long before he arrived. The trooping of the colors was included in this dramatic ritual of events before Hitler ever spoke one word. It was important, too, that there not be enough room for all the people in the assembly hall. Some of the crowd had to spill over onto steps and aisles. This gave the crowd, as a whole, a sense of packed togetherness with all of them waiting for the same major event. It was part of the total staging plan.

HITLER ARRIVES

Finally, after a long wait, the dramatic sound of drum rolls signaled that Hitler was about to come through the doors of the hall in seconds. He would walk in, and thousands of people would immediately leap to their feet, almost breathless from their keyed-up energy, tenseness, and excitement. Many of them yelled "Hitler," as if relieved that he was finally there.

Hitler would then proceed to give his speech. He used plenty of emotion in his speaking, talking about the hard times of the German People, nationalism, what had to be done for Germany to take its rightful place as a "master-race," as he put it, and what he was going to do for them.

His voice ranged from a raving pace to a deeper-toned, dramatic style. He had variety as a speaker and used it well. He knew how to wring every ounce of emotion from a speech. Many in the crowds would be almost limp from the experience of hearing and seeing him. Few surpassed him as a mob psychologist and expert stage manager. One can only wonder how many positive things Hitler could have done for Germany if he had used his powerful speaking abilities and stage management for good rather than evil.

NEWSCASTER HOWARD BEAL

Anger can be a strong emotion. An example of what anger can do is the character in the novel and film titled "Network." Newscaster Howard Beal has his television audience in the palm of his hand. He succeeds admirably in getting a great many of the viewers to go to their windows, stick their heads out, and yell that they are "mad as hell and are going to do something about it."

PRESIDENTS, SENATORS, AND CONGRESSIONAL REPS

Some presidents and leaders in congress, whatever the year or era, have the ability to stir the emotions of listeners. Such ability can become part of their power and enable them to stay in office, influence the passing of new bills and legislation, and sometimes either help, or hinder, the growth of the nation.

The royals in England and leaders in Japan, Canada, France, Germany, Ireland, Italy, Australia, and other countries have a similar power via their ability to speak well, communicate, and lead others.

HOW FAR CAN YOU GO AS A SPEAKER?

A college coach once refused to let actor Karl Malden go into acting. He would not let Malden appear in a school play. This made Malden even more determined. He went on to carve a highly successful career of playing character roles on the stage and screen. Malden won critical and popular praise for his work in such films as "Patton," "On the Waterfront," and the hit television series "Streets of San Francisco." Malden won an Academy Award for his best supporting actor performance in "A Streetcar Named Desire." You will learn in this book that you can certainly be a more effective speaker and communicator. You will see positive examples of quality communication, and you will find out how to plan and organize a speech and the nature of the major types of speeches.

You will be guided on how to develop into a speaker who not only has something to say, but who also says it well.

During the dark days of World War II, the great British leader, Winston Churchill, was visiting a school classroom. It was thought that he meant to say something cheerful to the students of that grim era. Yet the thought of the Germans and what they were then doing to England so enraged Churchill that he suddenly slammed his cane over an empty desk in the room and shouted to the startled students: "Never give up. Never never never never never give up!"

I say to you not to give up on the idea and goal that you can become a more confident and effective public speaker. You will find the way in this book. Your increased ability and power as a speaker/communicator may well change your life.

2

TELL-TALE SIGNS
OF POOR SPEAKERS

One proven way to learn is to see or discover what *not* to do. This is also true in speaking. By knowing the clear signals, or signs, of poor speakers, you can then avoid using them or letting them become bad habits in your own presentations before a group or audience.

Let's zero in on each type of poor speaker, so you will know what not to do.

THE SPEAKER WHO REPEATS "AND AH"

You can eliminate this trap by careful rehearsal of your talk or speech. Tape-recording your speech, or doing a video of it, and then listening/watching yourself will reveal whether you are guilty of this habit. Knowing your speech material well is the best insurance against too many "and ahs."

THE SPEAKER WHO CANNOT SLOW DOWN

The words of such speakers come out a mile a minute. One excellent way to solve this bad habit is to have a friend, or member of your family perhaps, listen to your speech. Ask whoever hears you to pay special attention to your rate of speaking.

Working to improve your rate of delivery takes some effort, and requires you to go over your speech time and again to correct a too fast a delivery, but it is well worth the effort. Try for a medium rate without speaking too slow or too quickly. The result is an audience that will not miss what you have to communicate.

THE SPEAKER WHO USES NO GESTURES, PAUSES, OR VARIETY

The best way to insure that your material has plenty of variety in it, plus an adequate number of gestures and pauses, is to plan your speech with these key elements in mind and then double-check them when recording your material.

Strive not to say everything in the same way, for it can drive an audience to distraction. Your voice, for example, can be low in some spots and louder or more powerful, more forceful, in other places. Work out a number of gestures you plan to use well in advance. If you do this and then practice your speech or talk enough, you will know automatically when and where to use each gesture.

THE SPEAKER WHO BOBS BACK AND FORTH

This is a sign of either a poor speaker or fear on the part of the speaker. To avoid bobbing on your feet while speaking, plant both feet on the floor with not too much space between them. Check at different times during your speech to be certain that both of your feet are on the floor and that you are not bobbing back and forth.

THE SPEAKER WHO READS EVERY WORD

Doing this turns a speech into a reading. Reading is simply not communicating with an audience. The worst thing about it is that eye contact between speaker and audience is destroyed and totally absent.

The only way to avoid reading a speech is to practice it to the point of knowing the material so well you do not have to lose audience contact.

In truth, it irritates and even angers some members of an audience when a speaker reads all or most of their material. It shows an audience that you, the speaker, did not think enough of them, or the occasion, to prepare.

No audience should be expected or asked to follow a speech, to keep up with it, when the speaker is reading it with head down for the most part.

Going over your speech or talk enough times, which means practicing it from start to finish again and again, gets the material registered in your mind and memory. Then you have only to glance occasionally at the material to continue with confidence and effectiveness.

NERVOUS JITTERS

The frightened or nervous jitters speaker may stimulate some sympathy in an audience at first, but most listeners will sooner or later wish the speech or talk was a shorter one. Or they may be sorry they are captive members of the audience.

The only cure for the speaking jitters is to develop confidence and ability via practice. I suggested this once to several extremely nervous speakers at a U.S. Navy base. A few of the students, however, lived aboard an aircraft carrier with 5500 other men and women. How could they practice and where?

I finally came up with the idea that they could go to the flight deck, the top deck of a carrier, either late at night or very early in the morning when few others would be around. They could then find a corner of the carrier, forward or aft, to practice their speech material out loud.

Several navy students tried this and found it worked. They said it was much better than trying to go over their speeches in their compartments, where they lived on the ship. I was pleased and a bit amazed that several of them put this practice idea into action on the flight deck.

SPEAKER'S VOICE TOO SOFT

When a speaker's voice is too low, it can drive an audience up the wall trying to hear what is being said. The same is true if the speaker's voice is too high or nasal, meaning that it sounds like the voice is coming out the nose.

An excellent way to learn to speak louder is to get up on a stage when nobody is around. Then have a friend or family member stand at the back of the theater, behind the last row of seats, and listen to you speak from the stage. See if you are being heard.

The idea is to raise your voice pitch level (or lower it, as the case may be) and go over your material until the person behind the last row can hear you.

The goal here is voice projection, and the only way to achieve it is via practice.

It can also help to read from news or weather reports, pretending you are a radio or television reporter. This can be done at home. Strive again and again to raise the level or volume of your speaking voice so that everyone in an audience will be able to clearly hear you.

WILL IT EVER END?

Finally, there is the speaker who never comes to an end. The way to avoid this problem is to time your material. Then you will know almost exactly how long it will run.

Some ministers, senators, politicians, and others seem to ramble on and on like it was their last public speech. In contrast, a popular Presbyterian minister in Florida rarely preaches more than ten minutes. He is so well-prepared that he has evidently developed the ability to say it all, to communicate his sermon, within a maximum of ten minutes. His congregation appreciates it and so do visitors.

A basic formula for speaking almost anywhere, although it's over-simplified, is worth keeping in mind whenever you speak to any group or audience:

1. Tell them first what you're going to tell them.

2. Next, actually tell them.

3. Finally, tell them what you have already told them.

Although this sounds a bit like double-talk, it does have reason behind it. Your introduction is telling them what you are about to say; it's a preview. Then, when you actually tell them, give them the meat of the material, you are communicating the body or main part of what you have to say. Finally, you summarize by telling the audience what you just told them.

Believe it or not, some speakers do very well indeed following this basic, if very simple, formula.

Above all, make sure that all three steps do not go on or last for too long. Knowing when to stop, and not straining an audience by speaking too long, is the sign of a smart speaker. This type of speaker gets invited back again and again.

3

OVERCOMING STAGE FRIGHT: THE FEAR OF SPEAKING

The fear of speaking to any group or audience, or the nervous jitters at the thought of it, is better known as stage fright. You must not let this fear keep you from becoming a dynamic speaker.

There are clear and basic reasons for this fear. First, understand that a great many people have it, so there is no reason to be ashamed about it. In fact, most speakers do better because of at least a small amount of nervousness.

Some of the world's finest actors, communicators, and celebrities have admitted they get nervous. Many of them claim that being keyed up helps them to give a better performance.

Some basic reasons for too great a fear of speaking include the following:

1. The fear of getting up in front of strangers

2. The fear of making a mistake and looking like a fool

3. The fear of your mind going blank—of forgetting what comes next in your speech.

4. The fear of just not measuring up in the eyes of those you
   know.

THE MIND GOES BLANK

Stage fright can cause a speaker to forget what comes next.
The person freezes, or the mind goes blank with one look at the
strange or even known faces in the audience.
When and if stage fright causes such a blank for you, a
wipeout, do not panic. A long pause (though not too long) can
give you a chance to recover, pick up the threads of your speech,
and get back on track.

The best way to counter stage fright, to even head it off
before it should strike, is to know the ideas and content of your
speech well enough to paraphrase the material if necessary; say
and communicate it in a different way, but still your own.

If you know the ideas behind the words of your speech, the
thoughts of it, it is always possible to get the material across in
a variety of ways.

Another choice open to you is to summarize what you have
already covered. While you are doing this, you can make a decision on how to proceed from there.

SOME NERVOUSNESS IS NORMAL

Keep in mind that some degree of nervousness is normal
and to be expected. professional actors, those who give television news reports, stage, radio, and screen performers, and mas-
ters of ceremonies all report some amount of nervousness or the
jitters.

In truth, some of this fear can help a speaker to do well. If
stage fright persists at the chronic level, however, that is when
a speaker needs help.

Here is a paradox about skill in public speaking. It is ranked
in first place, and the top factor, in helping college graduates

(and many others as well) obtain employment, yet 70 percent cite giving a speech as one of their greatest fears.

Other fears such as a blind date, job interview, formal dinner party, first day on a new job, meeting a date's parents, and being asked personal questions in public were all rated as lesser fears below speechmaking.

Compare presenting a speech with swimming. If the parent takes the child to the swimming pool on the first day of summer, and throws the child into the water, the fear of water may never leave the infant. By contrast, if the child is given swimming lessons several times a week, that child is very likely to be over any fear and able to swim by summer's end.

Here is a useful checklist of proven ways to get over stage fright and affect a cure from it:

1. Practice your speech or presentation enough so you feel confident that you know the material.

2. Be sure you know the ideas and thoughts behind your speech sections. Then if your mind goes blank for any reason, you should be able to paraphrase the information and put it into your own words.

3. Practice your speech in front of a waist-length mirror or full mirror. This always helps.

4. Seek feedback on your speech (and how you present it) from a family member, relative, friend, or neighbor. Ask them to listen to your presentation and offer constructive advice and suggestions on how to improve it.

5. Tape-record or videotape your speech or sections of it. By hearing your voice and possibly seeing yourself, you will learn much quicker what you are doing

wrong. You may, for example, be reading too much of the material, or keeping your head down too long, speaking at too fast a rate, bobbing back and forth on your feet, or whatever. When you tape record or videotape your presentation, then play it back several times while taking notes on what appears or sounds bad. These notes on how to upgrade your overall presentation can be very helpful.

6. Listen carefully to well-known or effective speakers. You can learn from them. Be alert when you hear teachers, politicians, network news reporters and anchor stars, ministers, motivational speakers, and others communicate via the spoken word. Hearing the better ones among them will also inspire you to become a more skillful speaker yourself.

7. Offer to speak whenever possible. The more you stand in front of an audience or group, and communicate, the less stage fright you will have. Speaking frequently builds your confidence and reduces stage fright.

PART
II

HAVE SOMETHING
TERRIFIC TO SAY

4

HAVE SOMETHING GREAT
TO COMMUNICATE

One element in your speaking presentations can make an enormous difference and virtually guarantee that most, if not all, of your audience will stay with you. I call this element the quality factor. What this means is that by having something dynamic and terrific to say, you will please your audience so much they will hope to hear you again.

So how do you get this quality factor into your speech and other presentations? You seek a captivating subject for your presentation and one that fits the audience you are addressing.

In the first place, do not choose a subject that is too technical or scientific unless, of course, you are speaking to rocket scientists or otherwise knowledgeable people on that subject.

The average listener has no trouble keeping up with from three to five main points in the middle, or body, of your speech. If you use more than five main points, many of your listeners will tune out or lose interest in your presentation. Too many main points complicate the communication process. This is the main reason that many spoken presentations often present only three or four key points.

A GUIDING PRINCIPLE
FOR YOUR PUBLIC SPEAKING

It's easy to tell when a speaker seems to be bored with his or her own material. The voice lacks power and enthusiasm. The speaker reads too much of the speech or presentation. There are no gestures, too little eye contact with the audience, or perhaps too slow or fast a speaking rate.

Actually, there are two basic types of speakers. One type of speaker has something to say. He or she is alive with vitality and eager to share the information, presentation, or speech material with the audience. The other type of speaker *has* to say something, meaning it comes across to the audience as being a chore, duty, something to get through on the part of the speaker. There is a world of difference between these two basic kinds of speakers.

Stay aware of this principle and let it guide you whenever you stand up in front of any group or audience. Make it your business to always have something to say that is of value, help, or interest to your audience. By so following this principle, you will demonstrate respect for your audience and their time. And your audience will know that you cared enough to prepare for the occasion, which will result in audience respect for you.

KNOW THE OBJECTIVE OF EVERY SPEECH

The goal or objective of each speech you give should be very clear. Most speeches and presentations fulfill one of the following goals:

- Inform
- Entertain
- Inspire
- Persuade

To inform an audience is to teach, impart information about

the subject, or perhaps explain how something works. Take the broad subject of time, for example. If you were to speak on this subject it would be like trying to swim the Atlantic Ocean. If you started to speak on time (the subject of time), you could still be speaking a month later. You need to narrow the subject of time down to a segment, or portion, you can deal with in a speech. You are looking for a central idea about time.

Think of yourself as a television camera zeroing in, coming in, for a close-up on the subject of time. What is an angle on this subject that you could handle? How about the central idea of how fast time goes by? This could work because it's narrowed much more than the wide topic of time.

The next step is to give your speech or presentation (on the subject of time) a specific title. How about using "The Only Time You Really Have Is Now." That is a long title and could be shortened to "Time Waits for No One" or perhaps "Time Is Fleeting." Once you know the central idea, you can brainstorm for possible titles. Here is what you now have:

Speech Subject: Time
Central Idea: How fast it goes
Specific Title: "Time Waits for No One"

To give you another example of this narrowing process, consider the subject of work:

Speech Subject: Work
Central Idea: Being your own boss
Specific Title: "The Self-Employment Picture"

You need to know the clear objective of each of the other speeches. They are:

Speech to Entertain: To amuse the audience
Speech to Inspire: To uplift the audience and possibly ennoble the subiect.

Speech to Persuade: To change either the lightly held views, opinions, and beliefs of the audience or their tightly held values and beliefs.

Once you know your objective for a speech, you simply move to the next step of choosing a suitable subject. Next you narrow the subject enough and finally you select a focused title.

A QUIZ TO HELP YOU

After each of the wide subjects listed below, find a central idea, a segment, portion, or angle on it. Then write down a likely specific title:

Subject	Central Idea	Possible Title
Money		
Marriage		
Sharks		
Real estate		
Music		
Politics		
England		
Weather		
Vacations		
Fishing		
Baseball		
Travel		
Canadian trains		
Western U.S.		
Taxes		
Health		
Europe		
Humor		
Sports		

5

FINDING THE BEST SUBJECTS FOR YOUR SPEECHES

Subjects for speeches, addresses, and informal talks are everywhere. Everything you do, wherever you go, your work, city, geographic section, vacation choice, your health, hobbies, relatives, family problems, and all other aspects of life hold potential ideas for speeches.

Let's look now at one of the most popular techniques for producing worthy speech ideas. It's called brainstorming.

BRAINSTORMING

This technique uses the list method. You simply write down the subjects that occur to you on a sheet of paper. Your list may include any number of wide topics. Here is what one brainstorming list might include:

Job hunting
Overseas travel
Flu shots
Quilts
Politics
Improving the school system

Stock market investing
Pubs in England
Paris restaurants
Today's FBI
Speed reading
Zoos
The Milky Way Galaxy
Driving defensively
Learning to speak Japanese

Obviously, it takes no genius to simply brainstorm a list of subjects. Here is a very useful clue that can save you time and effort in your choice of a suitable subject:

Subject Clue: Whenever you seek a subject, make it a point to pick one that truly interests you. Why? Simply because you will usually do a better job of communication if a given subject is of personal interest.

Why pick a subject that bores you out of your skull? If you focus on this clue, your list of possible subjects will be a shorter one and will reflect those subjects most worthy of your consideration.

If you are genuinely interested in computers, for example, then some segment of that overall topic would be a good choice for you.

This leads us to another important clue that you should always follow when planning any kind of oral communication:

Focus Clue: Simply stated you should always narrow down a wide subject to a segment, an angle on the broad subject, and something you can handle.

Take the wide subject of travel, for example. Travel is too broad a subject, too wide in scope, to use. You would still be speaking a month or so later and very likely six months later on the subject of travel. What about travel? It needs to be narrowed down to something you can manage.

The way to do this is to pretend you are a television or

movie camera. Come in for a "close-up angle" on the wide subject of travel. Here are some possible angles on travel, and other wide subjects, that could work. Notice how much more focused the angles are:

Wide Subject	Focused Angle
Travel	"The Best Way to See London"
Sports	"What It's Like to Coach the Jaguars"
Money	"How to Invest in Common Stocks"
Health	"The Vitamin C Craze"
Patriotism	"What the Flag Means to Me"

WHERE TO FIND SPEECH SUBJECTS

You have a number of sources to choose from when seeking possible subjects. Consider the following ones:

Newspapers
Books
Magazines
Newsletters
The Internet
Lists and indexes such as *Reader's Guide to Periodical Literature*
Television
Databases
Directories
Booklets
Pamphlets
Government publications
Parks
Travel agencies
Your own personal knowledge
Interviews you conduct
Materials via mail order
Electronic indexes
Walking through library stacks

Lectures
The traditional card catalog (now usually on computer)
Indexes of periodicals
Company publications
Dictionaries
Atlases
Books of quotations
Yearbooks
Almanacs

There is of course a real difference in having something
solid to say and just having to say something. The first idea
means that you are interested in the subject. The latter means that
you have to get up and say something just to get through it.
There is a big difference then in these two types of speakers.

TRADITIONAL SOURCES FOR SPEECH SUBJECTS

Keep in mind that how good a subject turns out to be often
depends on how well the material for it is handled.

Some subjects for speeches are better than others. What you
seek as a speaker is the best subjects for you. Various factors
already cited will have an influence on your choice of subject
and central idea.

The time and place of your speech, the interest areas, age,
education level, and general background of your audience, length
of your speech, and other considerations must all be considered.

Here are some traditional sources of subjects for speeches:

1. Your own personal experience: You are the most
   interesting person in the world, so do not forget your
   own past years and experiences as rich sources of
   possible ideas. Your former schools, travel, jobs,
   military service, and so on are just a few examples.

2. Remarks by and conversations with friends, family members, and relatives: A chance remark by anyone can lead you to good ideas for speeches.

3. Magazines: Any and all kinds of magazines are a natural source of up-to-date subjects. There are hundreds of new magazines every year on all manner of interest areas. Take health alone, for example. With the international craze and renewed interest in good health, many new magazines are focusing on this area.

4. Newspapers: There is a huge gold mine of good speech and short talk subjects in a variety of newspapers. Don't overlook the smaller and community newspapers. Overseas newspapers are also loaded with good ideas. Whenever you spot a likely subject, or focused central idea for a speech, cut it out and file it for future reference.

5. Books: Past and present books hold many potential speech ideas.

6. Other speeches. This is an especially good source if you take advantage of the chance to hear local and regional speakers in your area. You could do your own different version of the same subject or a related one.

7. Radio/Television: Something you see or hear on television may spark a strong speech idea. An inter view I once watched on the tube led me to an excellent idea for a speech about a major Civil War battlefield.

LIVE WITH YOUR TOP CHOICE AWHILE

After you choose the subject you like best, it's a good idea to kick it around in your mind awhile and live with it. Visualize yourself speaking on the subject and try to project or head off any possible problems with that subject. You may decide to select something else.

THE SPEECH OCCASION HAS AN INFLUENCE

If you happen to be speaking at a special time, say on the founding date of a club or group, perhaps on a national holiday, this would clearly have an influence on your material or subject choice.

You will usually know well in advance what day and time you will be speaking to an audience. There are times when this can change, as clubs, civic groups, associations, and other audiences sometimes have no choice but to change the time and date for a speaker to make a presentation.

It is also wise to adapt your introduction and speech material to overseas audiences. You might want to say something like this: "The last time I was in England, in winter, the jet stream was favorable resulting in delightful weather for February." If you have never been in the country where you are speaking, you would say something appropriate regarding that fact in your introduction.

UNIVERSAL HUMAN WANTS/DESIRES

To help you do well in choosing dynamic speech subjects, I'm listing below the universal specific wants or desires of people everywhere. By picking subjects that relate to these mass human desires, you will be much more likely to succeed in your speech presentation. The reason for this is simple. Audiences relate strongly to these wants, and if they detect that your speech or talk is connected with one or more of their desires they are much more likely to stay with you throughout your presentation.

Best of all, whenever you plan a speech or talk, long or short, look over this list of wants of the masses. They can lead you to subjects and add a great deal of practical power to your presentations.

Remember that the more of these human wants your speech relates to, or ties in, the better and more effective you will be as a speaker via the content of what you say. Here are the universal human desires and wants:

> To have more free time
> To be successful
> To be more creative
> To be praised
> To make money
> To escape physical pain
> To gratify curiosity
> To be in style
> To satisfy one's appetite
> To take advantage of opportunities
> To attract the opposite sex
> To be healthy
> To be clean
> To enjoy yourself
> To be self-confident
> To be popular
> To have beautiful possessions
> To be appreciated
> To have security
> To save time

6

GRAB THEIR ATTENTION AND KEEP IT

The most important element in the art of public speaking is getting the attention of the audience. You might have the greatest speech, address, or talk known to man, but if you don't grab audience attention at once you are usually dead in the water.

A college professor fired a gun during a class and then immediately asked each of his students to state what they were thinking about at the precise moment the gun was fired. Some were thinking about lunch. Others were thinking about various problems, still others were thinking of their plans for the approaching weekend, and the rest, the smallest number, were following what the professor had been saying.

The above example is clear proof that audiences may look like they are present, but in truth their minds may be miles away and focusing on a variety of other things. This is why any and every public speaker must open with something dynamic and strong enough to command the attention of listeners.

Success in gaining audience attention creates confidence in a speaker, so it is vitally important to master the methods of hooking audience attention.

PROVEN WAYS TO GRAB THEIR ATTENTION

There are a number of sound ways to lasso an audience and make sure they listen to you. Consider the following:

1. Open with a startling statement.

"Ninety-five percent of all Americans will not have enough money when they reach retirement." Keep your statement, the one you decide to use, connected with your subject. Simply look for some hard-hitting opening that will hook them.

2. Open with a quote.

"I cannot live without books," said Thomas Jefferson. This would be a strong opening when speaking on the subject of continuing to learn, or reading competence, and other similar subjects.

3. Dramatize your opening.

"The piano her late husband had loved to play so much now remained closed." Such a dramatic opening line would grab the attention of most in an audience.

4. Start with an intriguing question or series of questions.

Is eating cholesterol bad for you? Cholesterol is an important component of every cell in your body. It is so necessary to health that 80 percent of the cholesterol in our bodies is made by the liver. If cholesterol is so important, why is it considered bad? Or is it? You get the idea here I'm sure. Hit them with one, two, or three strong opening questions, and you can have them riveted to what you say next.

5. Use a personal reference or greeting.

This can sometimes work well and especially when you have a personal connection with the subject of your speech.

6. Use an example or anecdote.

When author Robert Louis Stevenson emerged from his bedroom with a manuscript, his wife read it and criticized it. Enraged, Stevenson threw the manuscript in the fire. "You're right," he said. He promptly returned to his bed and wrote almost around the clock for the next three to four days. This time he came out with a manuscript that was published as the 149 page classic titled *The Strange Case of Dr. Jekyll and Mr. Hyde*.

7. Use a reference to the occasion.
Would it not be a happier era if every day could be like Christmas?

8. Reference to an earlier speech.
The last time I spoke to you the Berlin Wall was standing, still intact.

9. Use a poem or poetry excerpt.
"Gather ye rosebuds while you may" is one example.

10. Humor, if in good taste, can be an effective way to grab audience attention.
"If I die, you'll find my wife at Walmart." In addition to one-liners, you might tell a humorous story or experience if suitable for the subject and in good taste.

There are some other ways to grab attention, but the above ten are some of the most popular ways to introduce a speech, address, or talk. The first impression an audience gets of a speaker is crucial and may well determine if members of that audience will listen to you or not.

MAINTAINING GOOD EYE CONTACT
WITH YOUR AUDIENCE
Al Jolson, one of the greatest entertainers of the early part

of the twentieth century, realized early in his career that singing "was no good if you couldn't see the faces of the audience." Singing was simply no good for him unless he could see the people in the audience. By the same token, a good speaker has the ability to maintain good eye contact. Speakers who look away from their listeners, glance out the windows or read their material, simply lose most of their audiences.

The next question than, is how does a speaker keep good eye contact? The one word answer is "practice." Cliché or not, "practice does make perfect" or closer to it. How can one become great, a true champion, in any art or discipline without the necessary practice? A speaker unwilling to practice will not go very far as a public speaker. Reading a speech word for word, or close to it, simply lifts the entire presentation out of the speaking arena and turns it into a public reading.

Experts claim there are 250,000 different facial expressions. Audiences want to see your facial expressions and have you look them in the eye as you present your spoken material. Can you imagine a sales manager reading to his or her sales team? No way. If it was done, many on the sales team would lose respect for the manager.

There are times when students giving speeches, and older adults as well, use the chalk or blackboard too much in their presentations. Do not misunderstand. It is fine to use the blackboard if you do it in a limited way. What becomes bad communication is when a speaker, any speaker, makes too much use of the board. You can probably guess why. Too much use of the board, and writing on it, causes the back of the speaker to be turned to the audience. In other words, eye contact with the audience is lost when a speaker's back is toward the audience for too long.

BE READY FOR THE UNEXPECTED

This quality comes with experience, but there are some guidelines that will help any speaker, new or experienced, to land on the feet.

When you know you are going to be speaking at a given place, it makes good sense to go there in advance and check out the room, assembly hall, conference room, auditorium, or wherever the presentation is to be made. Find out if possible how noisy the place may be, the quality of the acoustics, how large the audience might be (judging from the size of the hall or perhaps how many chairs are there), if airplanes go overhead every so often, or fire engines, or whatever. Such advance knowledge is extremely helpful to any speaker. Skilled and professional speakers always do such advance investigation, and it helps them to plan a stronger presentation.

TEST ATTENTION LEVEL OF OTHERS

The next time you find yourself part of an audience, look at the faces of people in the crowd around you. Try to determine how many of those near you are really listening with their full attention.

The truth is that many people usually tune out a speaker for varying degrees of time, depending on who the speaker is, how well he or she succeeds in hooking and keeping their attention, and how interested they may be in the subject.

I once had a memorable experience at a patriotic Fourth of July program. The scene was a football stadium in Atlanta, Georgia. Soon after the program got underway, with parades and speakers taking part on the stadium grounds below, a fight suddenly broke out in the crowd at the 45-yard line. More and more people became involved in the fight, and it was spreading fast. Something had to be done quickly. Police got to the scene fast, but they could not seem to get it under control. Too many were already fighting.

Then an interesting thing happened. The band began to play "The Star-Spangled Banner." Almost like magic, everyone stood up, and all who had been fighting stopped at once as if on cue. The national anthem did in an instant what all the police there that day could not do. What happened that afternoon made a strong impression on me.

I am not suggesting you perform the national anthem (of any country) when and if you lose audience attention while speaking. It does show that there are ways to regain attention. What every strong speaker needs is some methods for regaining the audience. Try not to lose your audience in the first place, but if you do, keep the following options in mind for they are proven and will work:

1. Say something startling or very dramatic. If your audience has tuned out, you will have to repeat it a few times before they take it in and respond with new attention.

2. Try a long pause. This abrupt silence may well rivet their attention anew on you and your speech.

3. Move out to the side of the podium (or lectern) or take a few steps away from where you've been speaking. Some speakers never move a foot throughout an entire speech or talk. Even some well-known speakers move to the front and side of the podium for variety. It can help to regain attention.

4. If you happen to be near or on a strong point in your speech, pound your fist or hand on the podium. Many may disagree with this method, but I have seen it work on a number of occasions. You need only pound once or twice to regain attention.

5. Use a dramatic or sweeping gesture. This is a visual tool worth trying. It works best for speakers who do not use many gestures when speaking. Seeing a sudden wide gesture (made with your arms or hands) will be like a flag-raising in the eyes of your audience and may thus call their immediate attention back to your speech.

6. If you have reached a point in your speech close enough to a question-and-answer period, assuming you have planned or can handle questions, you could open up your program to specific questions from your audience. There are listeners in almost every audience who welcome the chance to ask questions about the topic. If you suddenly resort to this option, keep in mind that you may have to skip important material you had originally planned. You may not have enough time left in your program to open it to questions.

7. Resort to a specific visual aid of some kind such as posters, charts, signs, drawings, film, slides, or any visual-aids at all. They can often help a speaker to regain lost attention. One picture is still worth a thousand words, to use an old cliché.

PLAN YOUR OPENING CAREFULLY

Since hooking attention right at the start of your speech is so crucial, you need to plan your beginning with care. Ask yourself the following questions:

• Is there some type of surprise or dramatic beginning you can use?

- What is the very first thing you can open with in your talk or speech that will rivet their attention?

- Would a key question or series of questions about your topic get audience attention?

- How can you make your introduction appealing and different? For help with this one, study and listen carefully to the openings used by other speakers. Take note of especially strong openings you hear. Why were these speakers so successful in getting attention? Perhaps you can use a similar technique in your own introduction.

Whether your presentation is a fairly brief talk, a medium length address, or major speech, it is absolutely imperative that you have an attention-getting beginning. Otherwise you may lose your audience fast, and that means the rest of your presentation will not get over to many or most in the audience.

7

STRIVE FOR VOICE VARIETY

Since your voice is the means by which you transmit the ideas and content of your speech, it is quite important in the achievement of a high level of communication quality and effectiveness.

Some speakers can be irritating to listen to because of a variety of vocal reasons:

1. The speaker mumbles. One reason this happens is simply because the speaker keeps his or her mouth nearly closed. You can prove this to yourself. Try to say something with your mouth almost shut. The result is a mumble and a very gargled one.

2. The speaker's pace is too fast or slow. Speaking like you are rushed not only fails to get across to an audience; it leaves listeners bewildered from trying to follow you. On the other hand, a very slow rate of delivery becomes so monotonous that your audience may not be able to hold out until the bitter end. Try for a medium rate of delivery, with variety of course, but not too fast or slow.

3. The over-use of "and a" or "and er." This grates on the nerves of an audience. It may be a sign that the one doing the speaking did not prepare for the speech or needs to develop more skill in presentation.

4. The purely boring voice is one with no life to it, no force, enthusiasm, or color. Such a voice makes the members of an audience wish they were anywhere but there listening to the talk. A flat, dull, and cold voice creates boredom. As a speaker, you are not addressing the wall; the members of an audience have a right to expect your voice to be vibrant and alive.

5. Words and syllables become garbled by a speaker. Listeners want to hear the words and syllables of sentences uttered or spoken clearly and distinctly—not half omitted or snarled in transmission. Strive to beam them out to your audiences as clearly as possible.

VOICE VARIETY IS A MUST IN SPEAKING

There is no doubt about it. Voice variety helps to please an audience and makes them want to keep listening to the speaker. Here are specific ways to get more variety in your own voice:

• Vary the rate of voice force you use.

• Vary your rate of speaking.

• Vary the pitch level of your voice. Try dropping, that is lowering, your voice at appropriate times and then raising it in other places.

A voice can even do much to establish a certain kind of image. The late and great actor Vincent Price believed this was why he had been cast so often in horror type films: "For some reason my voice has a timbre that evokes mystery, melodrama, and horror. I suppose the fact that I'm tall and speak with a theatrical voice contributes to my association with the occult." Author Lucile F. Aly describes the masterful effects of John G. Neihardt's poetry reading performances: "He prolongs his vowels in stressed words, and his singing quality added dignity to the rhythm of the lines. His only training (for reading poetry aloud) was shouting poetry into the wind as he walked back roads in Nebraska. He understands well the value of a pause, and his excellent phrasing also included the much less common practice of increasing the rate on unimportant words after a pause. The combination of lengthened vowels, pauses, and quickened rate on unstressed words lended variety to the fairly long lines."

There's a way you can prove the importance of voice variety to yourself. For a solid week or longer, try saying *everything* in the same way, in the same tone, the same pitch level, and at the same rate or pace. You will drive not only your friends and associates to distraction but also yourself.

Audiences expect to hear variety and rightly so. Another way to prove this to yourself is to tape-record some speech material, saying it all in the same way, the same pace or rate of speaking, and the same tone level. Then listen back to it for as long as you can stand it.

Sometimes it really helps to record (or videotape) one or more of your speeches in a dull and lifeless way and then listen back to it. Having heard it presented this way then helps you to make more of an effort to practice enough and be able to present it in a professional way.

TAPE-RECORDING YOUR SPEECH IS A DISCOVERY

I urge you without reservation to tape-record one or more of your talks or speeches and especially when you are preparing a presentation. Hearing what you sound like on tape (doing your best of course) will teach you a great deal about what needs to be done to improve all aspects of your presentation. Each and every time you plan to present a speech, it would be smart to record the speech and then take notes on what you feel should be done to make it more effective.

By recording a speech several times, before its actual presentation before an audience, you can perfect many aspects of it and thus be much more prepared when the time comes to present it. Here are other values of tape-recording a speech:

- If you have never heard your voice before, it may surprise you. A great many people have little or no idea what they actually sound like.

- Working with a tape-recorder allows you to hear the improvements you make in a speech (in comparison of an early tape with a later one).

- It's easier to critique your own speech because you, in effect, can assume the role of one listener in an audience.

- As you strive to improve as a speaker over a period of months and years, you can play back earlier taped speeches and actually realize the skills you are developing. This can be quite encouraging to you. This comparison is your proof that you are advancing as a speaker and communicator.

- Tape-recording helps to pin-point any voice defects, as well as other weaknesses of your overall presentation (such as style, content, language, and so on).

THE BEAUTY OF PAUSES

Over the years, I have noted that most of the really fine speakers make very good use of pauses in their talks or speeches. I realized this after listening to such dynamic speakers as Norman Vincent Peal, Billy Graham, and others. There is something very effective about a pause when used in the right places. Here are some specific reasons for using a pause:

1. A pause will often dramatize the next thing you say. It puts a definite spotlight on your next sentence or idea.

2. A pause gives you a chance to catch your breath and collect your thoughts.

3. A pause gives the audience a chance to catch up with you.

4. A pause may well regain audience attention because the sudden silence focuses new interest on the speaker.

5. A number of pauses in any address or spoken presentation simply aids the communication process and separates main points or sections of your speech from others.

Voice variety makes a speaker much more interesting to listen to and enjoy. When you speak to your friends, family members, or neighbors, you don't say everything in just the same way with the same pitch level. There is variety in your voice. In a similar way, audiences appreciate speakers who take the time, in planning and practice, to instill variety in the pace, the pitch level, the use of enthusiasm, lowering and raising the voice in places, saying things at times in dramatic ways, and more.

Strive to get more variety in your presentations, and audiences will love you for it and invite you back again and again.

PART
III

PLANNING YOUR
PRESENTATION

8

THE FOUR WAYS
TO PRESENT YOUR SPEECH

An early decision every speaker must make, whatever the subject of their presentation might be, is what way to communicate it.

There are four key ways to give a spoken presentation. By trying each of the major methods of delivery, you can discover which one you prefer to use and like best.

Probably the best way of all to present a speech is to know it so well that you simply stand up on your two feet, look them in the eye, and present your speech.

The question is how many speakers really feel confident enough to speak this way? Many get the jitters just thinking about speaking with no notes, materials, or helps of any kind. Your decision to choose this way of presentation should depend on how much preparation time you can devote to the speech and the length of it. This means going over your material so many times that you feel you know it so well, very well indeed, that you feel completely confident and ready to go with it.

In other words, you do not memorize the speech; you just know it so well—the ideas and key points you wish to communicate—that you are convinced you can present it most effectively.

Let's take a look now at the basic four methods and see how the advantages of each can be used in your own speaking:

SPEAKING FROM NOTES

With this method, your speaking notes might simply be a list of directions to yourself. For example: "describe a Hawaiian sunset or dawn," or "give the Winston Churchill quote," or "summarize the speech by repeating the most important main points." The notes that speakers use range from key phrases to complete ideas to be communicated. The notes are just reminders you have in front of you, to glance at now and then during your talk or speech. Even short speeches may involve the use of some notes, which are usually brief phrases or lines, or perhaps a list of ideas to get across.

Notes for a speech or talk may range from very simple ones to elaborate pages of many details.

SPEAKING FROM MEMORY

Another way of handling a speech is to memorize it. You take nothing at all with you to the speaking platform; you depend fully on your ability to remember your speech material. It goes without saying that if you choose this method, you must be very sure that your memory won't fail you.

In some of my early speeches, I decided to try this method of delivery. In fact, at age ten I tried this method as a contestant in a national speech tournament. I can remember going over the material again and again in many weeks of practice. I took no notes to the podium with me, for by that time I felt confident I could do well. The happy result was that I won the national contest.

I must warn you, however, that I discovered some strange things about the human mind, even though I won the speech contest on the importance of temperance for youth and in life. I learned that the human mind can suddenly go blank at any time. There were several occasions during my speech when my mind went absolutely blank. What did I do? How did I handle it? I ad-libbed. In other words, I simply said the material in a different way.

What came to my aid, even though I was forced to ad-lib several times, was the fact I had practiced so much that I knew the sections, thoughts, and key ideas of the speech well enough to be able to put it into different words at several places while keeping the integrity and same essential information of the speech intact.

Some individuals have photographic minds or simply the ability to memorize well, but these people are few and far between. There are not a great number of them. Generally speaking, I do not recommend you use the memory method unless you are one of these rare persons who memorizes well. Most of us do not. Even after all the time, effort, and work I spent on that speech at ten years old, I was horrified each of the several times during the speech when my mind went totally blank.

Something as simple as an airplane flying over the place where you are speaking can make your mind go blank. Perhaps an ambulance goes by somehow taking your memory with it. Someone in the audience might cough or sneeze and bam, your mind has gone blank, forcing you to ad-lib until you can get back on track. The memory method has its perils and hazards.

For those few but fortunate people who have great memories, or the ability to memorize material well, this method is a great one. Why? because once a speech is memorized, the speaker needs nothing else. He or she walks to the podium with no notes, no manuscript, or anything else but the intact speech in his or her memory.

For most speakers, however, again I do not recommend this method.

SPEAKING FROM FULL MANUSCRIPT

One method that many speakers like is the full manuscript technique. Here you write out your speech or talk word for word, section by section, and carry this entire manuscript with you to the podium.

With this method, if and when your mind goes blank, you have your full speech right there in front of you. A full manuscript serves as your backup in the event you somehow lose track.

You can probably guess what the disadvantage of this method is for many speakers. Yes, too many speakers who use this method, end up reading far too much of their material. That means, of course, that the speaker's head is down too much of the time and reading what comes next. Eye contact with the audience is thus lost for perhaps extended periods of time. You know what that means. It means poor communication and very possibly a bored, inattentive audience.

Eye contact with the audience is vitally important, and losing it too much is the risk you run with the full manuscript method.

Now I must qualify the above and say that once again there are certain speakers who have a strong ability to do well using a full manuscript. In other words, they practice so much, in spite of knowing they will have a manuscript right there, that they do not have to read the material. They do not have to look away from the audience for extended amounts of time.

So having a full manuscript is a good back-up, but it does not eliminate the need to practice the speech. Some speakers just want to know a manuscript is in front of them just in case of trouble.

I believe this method can work, providing the speaker does not read the material but practices enough to be able to communicate it to the audience while maintaining strong eye contact.

THE OUTLINE METHOD

Some consider this method separate, but I usually link it with notes, calling it the Notes-Outline Method.

Some outlines are elaborate plans with numerous headings and sub-headings; others are basically simple. If you like the idea of using an outline, decide to write a detailed one or go the simple route.

You may well want a more involved outline if your speech is a long and fairly technical one. If you decide on a simple form of outline, you might just list the essential points you wish to get across in the introduction, middle part, and conclusion of your speech.

You can also use the large letter, number, and small letter outline system, or just list what you intend to do in the three major sections of your speech. Perhaps you have a dramatic story to tell, as an introduction to your speech. If so, indicate that story on your outline under "introduction."

Example Introduction: Story on the increasing number of people who are combining vacations with business trips.

Simple Outline Example:

Introduction: Cite the need for additional sources of income today.

Middle part: Give main points and supporting materials for each.

Conclusion: Close with summary or effective anecdote/illustration.

Large letter, number, and small letter outline (Example):
A. Introduce speech by giving some of the most shocking crime figures.

B. First main point—Today's society is a violent one.
  1. Illustration of brutal murder of nurse in St. Louis.

a. Cite testimony of experts.
b. Give reasons for the crime.

One advantage of speaking from an outline is that you can often get all of it on a single page or two. Though it depends upon where you are speaking, it can sometimes present problems to use a full manuscript, memorize, or use only notes.

A one or two page outline may be easier to manage. It depends on one's individual preference. You should try these various methods of speaking for yourself.

THE EXTEMPORANEOUS METHOD

Most professional speakers and experts agree on another excellent way to present a talk or speech. In other words, they believe this method is the best one of all. It's called the extemporaneous method.

By extemporaneous, I do not mean that you stand up and speak without any previous preparation. That form of oral communication is referred to as *impromptu* speaking.

Here are the recommended steps of this ideal way to present a talk or speech. By using them as a guide, and perfecting the method, you will have the knowledge of what I'm convinced is the very best way to communicate with an audience:

1. Decide on the purpose and subject of your talk or speech. Set a title for it and think about what the material will consist of.

2. Plan the introduction and conclusion of your speech.

3. Select what three, four, or five (maximum) main points you will use in the middle of your speech and the supporting materials you will use for each one.

4. Find key examples, anecdotes, quotes, and statistics (if any) to back up your speech.

Before the day or evening of your talk or speech, type or write out on index cards the key lead line or phrase of each section of your speech. All you need to write on each card at the top (or in the middle) is a cue line or phrase. Then number the cards to keep them in proper order. The idea of this card system is simple. The one phrase or line on each card will serve as a beacon to remind you what comes next in your speech.

Next learn the material of your speech exceptionally well, and that means plenty of practice. You can do this by going over the material many times. The objective is to set up a pattern in your mind. Know what each section of your speech consists of and what thoughts or ideas are being communicated.

I do not mean that you memorize the material. Just know it well and what it essentially says. Know what it is you want to get across to your audience. By reading over the material many times you are certain to get familiar with it. Simply study and practice it so well that you feel confident about presenting it.

It can be most helpful to let a friend, family member, or relative listen to your speech. You do not have to give the material the same way you will before a live audience and you probably won't.

The idea of the extemporaneous method is that you know the material, the content, very well indeed, so well that the presentation of it takes care of itself.

On the day or night of your presentation, place your index cards on the podium or lectern in the order of your speech plan. Make sure the cards are secure and that nothing will get them out of order or knock them on the floor.

You are now ready to start your speech or talk. Here you will see the benefits of this method. You are introduced as the speaker. You rise and walk to the podium. The big moment has arrived.

You glance down at your neat stack of cards. The first one has only one phrase on it, which is all you need to see. Say, for example, you are speaking on the subject of being more creative. The phrase on your first card simply reads: "Introduce speech with Canadian pianist illustration." You have already prepared well. Reading the phrase triggers your mind, and you go right into the introduction.

After your introduction, you turn to the phrase or line at the top (or middle) of the next card. It reads: "Give examples of how the listener can become more creative." Once again, this is all you need to know. You then proceed with a series of examples telling how each listener in your audience has the potential power to become more creative.

As an example of support for one of your main points, when you reach that point in your speech, you simply look at the next card (still in order). The card might say something like this: "Give example of Birdman of Alcatraz and how he became an expert."

So it goes on through your talk or speech. The line or phrase, one only on each card, *triggers* your mind and you move forward in your speech until you have finished it.

Now you may not even need to look at the cards you have placed on the podium. You may know the thought, the idea content of your speech, so well that it is not necessary to glance away from your audience for even a moment. This is truly the extemporaneous method.

You simply know your material so well that you trust and have strong confidence that you will present it most effectively when the time comes. On the other hand, some speakers like to have the three-by five cards ready to glance at because they do serve to trigger your mind effectively.

As you finish a particular section of your speech (when using cue cards), you simply glance at the top or middle of the next card and continue. Think of these as cue cards or prompting cards.

Now consider these advantages of speaking this way via the extemporaneous method:

1. You don't have to worry about a loss of memory. Remember, you know your speech or talk essentials so well that you can communicate the ideas and thoughts in a number of ways, if necessary, and as your own style and personality direct.

2. Since you have only to glance at the lead line on each of your index cards, this method allows you to maintain excellent eye contact with your audience. As a result, the quality of the communication with your audience is much higher.

3. You need have no fear of losing your place in a speech manuscript because you do not have to bother with one. All you have is a stack of index cards with a lead line or phrase at the top of each one or on the middle of each. Each card will *trigger* your memory to move to the next thought or topic.

4. Your presentation seems quite natural and not wooden, canned, or artificial.

5. Because you know so well what you want to say, you do not have to worry about word order. Your presentation flows forward smoothly.

6. If a better way of communicating a certain point suggests itself, or comes to you while speaking, you can use it. In other words, you are not bound to a

rigid structure or word/sentence order. In fact, this sometimes happens in the extemporaneous method. The result is a more flexible and effective presentation.

7. This method of speaking will give you a great deal of confidence and enthusiasm in your ability to make successful speeches.

8. When your speech or talk is concluded, you have only to place the cards in order again to be ready to speak the next time.

The cue cards will establish grooves in your mind, and this is especially true if you give the same speech or talk a number of times. After a number of presentations, you may not even need the cue cards at all. You may discover that you can present your speech in ever new and fresh ways. You just stand up and say it all in a new and interesting way each time.

Again, I can vouch for this way of speaking. I have tried a full manuscript, an outline, and the memory plus various notes routes. This method of lead phrases or lines on index cards is by far the best method.

I urge you to try this extemporaneous way of speaking. You will like speaking this way and appearing before audiences. Your speeches and talks will have a marvelously fresh and natural quality about them. Audiences will want to hear you speak again and will invite you back.

9

GESTURES MAKE
A DIFFERENCE

Getting speech material across to an audience is sometimes difficult depending upon the nature of the subject, type of audience, and where you are speaking. A very useful and helpful tool for communicating to an audience is the gesture. It aids the communication process well.

It's interesting to consider what communication might be like if using gestures alone. The silent screen stars had to act this way for their movie roles before sound films came along and changed the industry.

Gestures help a speaker to express personality. Letting your hands and arms support what you are saying makes good sense. You want your gestures to be natural and not look forced. Some speakers also overdo gestures and may look like they are trying to wave a passing car by or are out of control.

Gesture is an art. It is an international language. The human hand alone uses levels, planes, and positions when communicating. A shrug of the shoulders is still used to mean something is unclear. A nod of the head usually stands for yes. The open hand, with palm showing, stretched out before a speaker still usually means stop.

HOW GESTURES HELP COMMUNICATION

The simple but effective gesture adds communication power to what is being transmitted to listeners.

- A gesture can help to clarify something, a confusing point.

- Certain gestures reveal the confidence and conviction of the speaker.

- A gesture can strengthen a basic statement.

- A speaker may sometimes look too lifeless and wooden, like a robot behind the podium. By just standing for the length of the presentation, with no gestures at all, the speaker loses vitality, enthusiasm, and power.

- Gestures can help a speaker describe something to an audience ("as tall as a bookcase," "big as a breadbasket," or "as long as from here to the back of this hall").

The above are all sound reasons for using gestures each time you stand before an audience. Again, you will find that in practicing your material you will learn where the best places are to use gestures. But remember, don't use too many gestures because it can become distracting.

WHAT TO DO WITH YOUR HANDS

Remember Fred Astaire? He was without doubt the greatest dancer of the century as well as a very able actor and singer. Yet the enormously popular star once stated in an interview that he was always bothered by his hands when dancing. He "always felt his hands were too large and they got in his way when dancing." What an incredible admission from one of Hollywood's greatest immortals.

Obviously, as time passed, Fred learned to not worry about his hands when dancing. It is very surprising to know that he felt this way and especially in the early years of his career.

Some speakers are bugged by both their hands and arms. They are never sure whether to keep them at their sides throughout their presentations or on the sides of the podium. There is one very helpful fact about the hand mike. It lets a speaker or master of ceremonies have something to do with their hands. One hand is busy clearing the trailing cord of the mike. The other hand is holding the mike.

The normal place for your arms when speaking is at your sides, but this does not mean they stay there, lifeless, for the entire presentation. It is fine to place your hands on the sides of the podium. It's also okay to move to one side of the lectern or podium for awhile. Variety is the goal here. Try to keep one hand and arm free, or both, for gestures that are natural, graceful, and that come in the right places of your presentation.

THE ARTFUL USE OF THE JAB

Back in Chapter One we flashed backed to John Kennedy's effective use of the jab when he spoke those famous words: "Ask not what your country can do for you." How much less effective would that highlight (of his Inaugural Address) have been without the artful use of the jab? He emphasized and empowered those words by jabbing the air in a diagonal way. The result was an unforgettable statement and memory of a speaker in action.

NEGATIVE VIEWS ON GESTURES

You should also be aware of the objections to gestures, so here are some of the most frequently voiced ones:

- Some gestures don't look natural. They appear to be forced or contrived, even though the speaker tries his or her best.

- Gestures are not positive proof of sincerity.

- Gestures look phony when used by a number of speakers.

- Too many gestures may be an attempt by the speaker to hide nervousness or the jitters.

- Gestures may be distracting to some people in an audience. This is especially true if the speaker goes overboard and uses far too many gestures.

- The audience may focus on the gestures of the speaker instead of the content and material of the talk or speech itself.

There are times when body movements other than planned gestures are very distracting to an audience.

I still remember hearing a North Carolina preacher who never gestured with either his hands or arms. He never moved to either side of the pulpit and rarely, if ever, moved a foot away while speaking.

One particular distracting habit of this Carolina speaker was the way he bobbed backward and forward on the heels of his feet. This went on for almost the entire length of the sermon. I noticed that many listeners seemed bored and inattentive to what he was communicating.

Perhaps this speaker did not realize that he bobbed back and forth while speaking, but he kept it up during the several times I heard him speak. Some arm and hand gestures plus a halt of the bobbing would have helped his communication process a great deal.

NOTES FORM OBSERVING SPEAKERS

Here are a few examples of speakers using gestures that I have observed:

1. The speaker at one point had his elbow on the podium which is a big no no.

2. This speaker needed to make wider gestures. The ones used were too narrow.

3. The gestures in this speech were very effective and covered the full range. This was a skillful speaker.

4. Good use of the yardstick to make gestures and to point out chart material used in the presentation.

5. She kept her arms behind her back most of the time. I only saw two gestures, and they looked forced.

YOUR OWN USE OF GESTURES

You should definitely plan to use at least some gestures in your talks. They will be better because of them.

If you discover that your hands want to do even more, and try to talk for you, try to control the urge to us too many gestures. If your hands are constantly involved in a variety of gestures, it may look overdone, forced, and artificial, depending on the overall ability and degree of skill you reveal.

In general, it's usually better to use fewer gestures that look and are genuine and sincere. When not overdone, the gestures you do use will be that much more meaningful and important.

10 _____

TECHNIQUES OF EMOTIONAL APPEAL

Aristotle, the Greek philosopher who wrote a masterful and definitive work on communication and its process, *Rhetoric*, believed that persuasion in every case is achieved by appealing to the emotions, giving the right impression of the speaker's character, and proving the truth of statements made.

Most people are reached via their emotions. Again a classic case in point is the rise of Adolf Hitler. He continually appealed to the patriotism and nationalism of the German people. He often focused on how badly Germany had been treated after World War I and how the destiny of Germany was to lead the world and fulfill its glorious place in history.

Your ability as a speaker to reach and stir the emotions can result in true oratory. I kid you not. Appealing to the emotions involves a sense of ethics for the wrong use of emotional appeals can result in abuse of power, evil, and destruction, as the example of Hitler proves. You have heard the saying often that "power corrupts and absolute power corrupts absolutely." It is true.

THE KEY EMOTIONS

What are some of these emotions. They are:

- Love
- Fear
- Hatred
- Freedom
- Friendship
- Pride
- Confidence

When England stood alone against the Nazi threat to their nation, before America had entered the war, it was one man alone who kept the British people united and determined to resist and be victorious. His name was Winston Churchill.

In the following speech excerpt, notice how Churchill appeals to the sense of freedom, the desire of the British people to be free, as well as how this great speaker artfully used the device of repetition:

> We shall not flag nor fail. We shall go on to the end, we shall fight in France, we shall fight on the seas and oceans, we shall fight with growing confidence and strength in the air, we shall defend our island, whatever the cost may be, we shall fight on the beaches, we shall fight on the landing grounds, we shall fight in the fields and in the streets, we shall fight in the hills, we shall never surrender.

A GREAT GENERAL RETIRES

When President Truman abruptly recalled General Douglas MacArthur from his post in the Far East, the famous general defended his conduct in a speech delivered before a joint session of Congress in April, 1951.

Perhaps the most memorable and often quoted line of

MacArthur's speech came near the end when the general de-
scribed how he still remembered the refrain of one of the most
popular barracks ballads of that day, which proclaimed that "old
soldiers never die; they just fade away. I will now just fade
away, an old soldier who tried to do his duty as God gave me the
light to see that duty. Good-bye."

Reactions to the speech were mixed. One sympathetic Con-
gressional hearer said: "We saw a great hunk of God in the flesh,
and we heard the voice of God."

Many felt that the speech was highly charged with emotion,
but how could it have been otherwise? One of the most brilliant
military generals of all time had been fired from his job and
brought home to lay down his military career, which no doubt
broke the old general's heart.

When a great military leader speaks before Congress and
sixty million or so Americans, to justify his life's work and
reputation, it seems only natural that such a speech would be
filled to the brim with emotion. I heard the speech and believe
MacArthur expressed his honest, heartfelt emotions. He was not
trying to manipulate the audience or appeal to their emotions in
any unethical way.

Gary Cronkhite, in an article for *The Quarterly Journal of
Speech*, defined emotion as "activation, or level of arousal."
Evaluating emotional appeal consists of estimating the sum of
the motivational strengths or the impact of the verbal stimuli
used to represent these motivational concepts.

Aristotle stated, in his *Rhetoric*, that the speaker's language
will be "appropriate if it expresses emotion and character and
does not speak casually about weighty matters, nor solemnly
about trivial ones." MacArthur certainly did not speak casually.
Most of the critics agreed that he spoke eloquently, and a study
of the speech reveals his strong character through the use of
language.

The emotions of *love* and *friendship* are quite evident in the
speech. Perhaps this can best be seen in a comment the general

made shortly before he gave his speech when he was asked about his politics. He replied: "The only politics I have is contained in a single phrase known well to all of you—God Bless America.'"

MacArthur's great love of country is a dominant emotion that can hardly be missed in the speech. He showed the audience he had love, that he was just, and he did so through his handling of the speech materials.

Words and ideas eloquently spoken and communicated to an audience have great power. Proof of it is the fact that after MacArthur's speech, many Americans urged him to run for the Presidency. The very opening, the introduction, of his speech revealed the humanity and pride, the friendliness, sincerity, knowledge of his subject, and his tremendous love of country. After all he had already done for the nation, he still wished to serve. Such devotion is bound to stir listeners: "I address you with neither rancor nor bitterness in the fading twilight of life, with but one purpose in mind: to serve my country." Duty, honor, country—that was his focus.

One of the key lines in the speech was: "In war there is no substitute for victory." The speaker, MacArthur, made it clear that he was for ending the then current Korean conflict as soon as possible, had a plan to do so, but was prevented from executing it. The implication was that our government leaders did not want victory.

The anguish and anxiety caused MacArthur by the bloodshed of the war was bound to have been felt by millions of listeners. Yet at the close of the speech, when he flashbacked to his oath at West point and the "old soldiers never die" quote, he was at the highest point of emotion.

In one of his very last speeches to the cadets at West Point, MacArthur said the following lines which must have stirred the cadets to the core of their beings: "And I want you to know that when I cross over the bar, my last conscious thought will be of the Corps...and the Corps...and the Corps."

SALES PROFESSIONALS USE
EMOTIONAL APPEALS

Ever think what might happen if the thousands of sales professionals simply stopped doing their thing? The economy would take a nosedive. No products or goods would be sold, and the business world would sink into rapid decline. Sales people move the products and goods of their nations, and in so doing they place themselves in the front lines of important speakers.

To persuade a prospect to buy, to sign on the dotted line and make payment, is persuasion in action. The use of emotional appeals when sales people communicate their product features, and reasons to buy, is often necessary. No doubt there are busy sales people who make use of emotional appeals without clearly realizing it. All they know is that they get the prospect to sign and buy the item.

HAPPINESS IS AN EMOTION

The American Constitution states very clearly that all citizens have "the right to life, liberty, and the pursuit of happiness." I once gave a speech involving this emotion of happiness, and I decided to tie it in with the listener's individual dream.

Most people, wherever they live and whatever they now do, have a dream or dreams they are trying to fulfill unless they have for one or more reasons given up on it. With this as my theme, I planned a speech that would hopefully inspire my audience *not* to give up on their dream but to do all in their power to move closer to it.

This was the way I introduced the speech, hoping very much that it would grab the attention of my audience:

Introduction

You've heard of vitamin power, money and political power, and so on, but have you ever thought about dream power and what it can do to change your life for the better?

Millions of people around the world discover sooner or later that even the security of a job, career, or profession is not enough.

A dream can change that empty feeling in your heart, fill you with renewed vigor, and give you an ongoing reason for making the most of your time on earth.

Body (Middle) of Speech

The middle of my speech went like this, though I have edited parts of it and am presenting mostly the key points that formed the body or middle part of the speech.

What can a dream do for you, should you not presently have one? Here are just a few of the advantages of having a dream in your life:

1. A dream gives you a purpose, a reason for being, an objective. (I then gave examples to back up this point.)

2. A dream stimulates your imagination and creativity. (Testimony, explanations, anecdotes, and other proof were communicated).

3. A dream keeps you more enthused about life in general. (More supporting materials were presented including quotes, descriptions, and more illustrations).

4. A dream motivates you to think ahead and plan for your future. (More examples and supporting materials were then used).

5. Having a dream you are determined to fulfill can keep you more healthy. Medical experts have proven that boredom can actually kill you. A dream keeps you alive and humming on all cylinders. (More support for this followed).

6. A dream enables you to get much more out of life in the way of personal satisfaction. (Examples,

quotations, and descriptions backed up this main point).

Please note that it's usually better not to use more than four or five main points in a speech. Most speeches and addresses limit the main points to three. Six points were probably one too many, but I went ahead with this plan, and the speech seemed to go well.

Conclusion

For my conclusion of the speech, I decided to focus on the important truth that dreams *do* come true.

Write these words in blazing red letters across the screen of your mind and in the central core of your being: DREAMS DO COME TRUE. Many people all over the world have experienced the unique thrill of realizing one or more important dreams in their lives. I see no reason why you cannot do the same.

Yet to achieve what you want, you must know what your dream is, build a very strong desire to achieve it, fan the flame of that desire, work out a sensible plan for the steps, or series of goals leading to your dream, and then apply your plan relentlessly plus updated, streamlined versions of your plan, regardless of the obstacles you may now see or see later in your pathway.

Remember the words of Henry David Thoreau: "March confidently ahead in the direction of your dreams, and you can reach an uncommon level of success."

I'll be betting on you and believing that you can and will make that dream in your heart a tangible reality. May you know that joyous moment of true happiness, the happiness of a dream fulfilled. There is nothing else quite like it.

11

THE POWER OF SINCERITY
IN SPEAKING

If you think about the most powerful speeches you have heard in your lifetime, you will agree that a major reason for their success was the sincerity of the speaker. Learn to get more sincerity into your talks and speeches, and you will be well on the road to compelling speaking.

Sincerity hits home with most listeners. Perhaps you feel that you have tried to be sincere in the talks and speeches you have already presented, but it's the degree of sincerity that is important. The truth is that most speakers could be more effective, by doing some serious thinking about sincerity and then developing more of it when they speak.

THE STUNNING DREYFUS SPEECH

Sincerity can take you far in public speaking. Every good speaker projects genuine sincerity. The powerful, dynamic type of speaker has a great deal of it and it comes across to audiences.

When French novelist Emile Zola spoke on February, 1898, to denounce the conspiracy against Captain Alfred Dreyfus, his speech was permeated with sincerity:

Dreyfus is innocent. I swear it! I stake my life on it—my honor! At this solemn moment, in the presence of this tribunal which is the representative of human justice, before you, gentlemen, who are the very incarnation of the country, before the whole of France, before the whole world, I swear that Dreyfus is innocent.

By my forty years of work, by the authority that this toil may have given me, I swear that Dreyfus is innocent. By all I have now, by the name I have made for myself, by my works, which have helped for the expansion of French literature, I swear that Dreyfus is innocent. May all that melt away, may my works perish, if Dreyfus be not innocent! He is innocent. All seems against me—the two Chambers, the civil authority, the most widely circulated journals, the public opinion they have poisoned. And I have for me only an ideal of truth and justice. But I am quite calm; I shall conquer. I was determined that my country should not remain the victim of lies and injustice. I may be condemned here. The day will come when France will thank me for having helped to save her honor.

EVERY TRUE ORATOR HAS SINCERITY

Winston Churchill was a unique speaker with a great deal of sincerity. People believed in him, and it was his great sincerity and determination in leading the British people through the dark days of World War II that made possible that nation's finest hour.

Note Churchill's sincerity when he presented his program in a speech on May 13, 1940:

To form an administration of this scale and complexity is a serious undertaking in itself, but it must be remembered that we are in the preliminary state of one of the greatest battles in history, that we are in action at many points in Norway and in Holland, that we have to be prepared in the Mediterranean, that the air battle is continuous and that many preparations have to be made here at home. In this crisis I hope I may be pardoned if I do not address the House at any length today. I hope that any of my friends and colleagues, or former colleagues, who are affected by the political reconstructions, will make all allowance for any lack of ceremony with which it has been necessary to act. I would say to the House, as I said to those who have joined this Government: I have nothing to offer but blood, toil, tears, and sweat.

Flashback to the House of Burgesses, in the Colonial Period, when the colonists were fed up with the control and demands of England. There were some good speeches that day but it was Patrick Henry who said it all in these compelling words. You can almost see him at the great historical moment on his feet and speaking with heartfelt sincerity and fire: "I know not what course others may take, but as for me give me liberty or give me death!"

WHAT IS SINCERITY?

The long and distinguished work of Billy Graham is a powerful example of sincerity in action. A big part of his power as a speaker is his great sincerity. "Sincerity is the biggest part of selling anything," Graham once said. People who hear the evangelist speak may not always agree with his religious views and statements, but few doubt the man's sincerity and that it is genuine.

Graham discovered the invaluable motivational power of sincerity one summer as a youth. He and a friend took their first jobs on their own working as traveling salesmen for the Fuller Brush Company.

Graham sold more brushes that summer than any other salesman in the entire state of North Carolina. "I believed in the product."

Believing in the subjects of your talks and speeches will increase your sincerity when presenting material before audiences. Naturally, if you believe in what you are saying, you are going to sound more sincere. It comes across to an audience.

Strive to know the subjects of your speeches intimately, for it will definitely help you to project sincerity. Churchill believed most deeply in the subjects of his speeches, and the great statesman's strong sincerity came across.

The sales manager of a given company believes in the product his or her team represents. So when that sales manager speaks to the members of the sales team, it sounds sincere because it is indeed sincere.

Billy Graham learned the art of projecting his enthusiasm into the promotion of his product that summer. In a similar way, if you can learn to project your own enthusiasm into your speaking, you will succeed in accomplishing the purpose of each speech you present.

How you really feel about what you say in your talks and speeches will get across sooner or later to audiences and especially if you present the same speech a number of times. The sincerity of a Churchill or a Billy Graham comes across in their voices, styles, and examples, which have a ring of strong conviction and sincerity about them.

Turn back to the Emile Zola speech section in this chapter and read it again. Even though you cannot hear his voice, there is a meaning, a substance, a gripping quality in the words and sentences themselves. Imagine what a powerful speech it must have been to hear on that day. He spoke in defense of an innocent man's life. Notice how many times Zola uses the line "I swear Dreyfus is innocent." Notice also how many times Zola stakes everything he has—his career, his works, great reputation, his very life—that Dreyfus is innocent. His sincerity that day did much to free an innocent man and save his life. It was a great and noble thing Zola did to defend and save Dreyfus. It also shows the tremendous power and good that public speaking can do. It shows, too, the power of sincerity in action. You could not find a better reason than this example for improving your own abilities as a speaker.

When students and mature adults wonder and ask why a person should study or try to develop skill as a speaker, I tell them about the Emile Zola and Alfred Dreyfus case. It says it all.

HOW TO GET MORE SINCERITY IN YOUR TALKS

Since genuine sincerity does so much to communicate to an audience, it's well worth the effort to instill more of it in your own speaking. Here are some proven guidelines for getting more of this dynamic quality into your speaking:

- Strive to project more enthusiasm in your overall presentation. Enthusiasm is contagious and often is equated with sincerity.

- Personalize some of your material, if the subject makes this possible. To personalize the material helps listeners to identify with it more.

- Whenever you hear good sincerity in a speech, note how the speaker seemed to inject this quality into his or her speech or talk.

- Use material in your speeches (key ideas, main ideas and points) that you really believe yourself. If you don't believe it, how can you expect an audience to do so? Most audiences can tell when and if a speaker is truly sincere.

- When you videotape or tape-record your speech, make sure your voice sounds sincere and that you are looking at the audience as much as possible. Work on these areas of your speech that do not seem to come across as genuine.

- Strive to bring new light on the subject of your talk. Let your audience hear and feel in their hearts your effort and desire to uplift the truth and ennoble the subject.

- Be certain you have some high quality examples and supporting materials to help drive home your main ideas and points. Some topnotch illustrations, anecdotes, quotes, descriptions, explanations, and examples will add to the heartfelt conviction and sincerity of your overall speech.

12

PRACTICE INCREASES YOUR SKILL AND CONFIDENCE

The reason most people do not develop confidence and skill as speakers is the lack of practice. I believe the golf champion Tiger Woods is a strong example here. Would Tiger be the champion he is today if he had not started using the clubs and hitting the ball as a very small boy? It's very unlikely.

Tiger's dad deserves a lot of credit for his son being a great golf pro today. His dad put the clubs in the little boy's hands and got him started. He grew up practicing and learning the right way to hit the golf ball.

There is no substitute for practice whatever the game, discipline, art, or skill involved.

Several of my U.S. Navy students caught fire with the idea of practice and used the corner of the flight deck of an aircraft carrier to practice. They, of course, practiced at early or late hours when few others were around. I believe this dedication shows that anyone can find or make time for practice if they really want to do so.

BE FRIENDS WITH THE SPOKEN WORD

How can a speaker truly become friends with the spoken word if he or she never gets up in front of a group and communicates?

A teacher of public speaking in Wales once encouraged one of his students, Richard Jenkins, to become friends with the spoken word. The young man did exactly that and got very interested in the dramatic end of the spoken word. The result was his rise to stardom as one of the world's leading actors by the name of Richard Burton.

There are a number of ways to become friends with the spoken word. You can trace the development of speech over the centuries. You can read what Aristotle said about rhetoric. You can learn how the elocution movement in this country and others grew. We have come a long way since the cave man era of communication via growls.

What else can you do? You can take a course in public speaking not just for three hours of credit but because you want to gain skill as a speaker. You can learn the difference between hearing and listening and discover why some speeches hold your attention much more than others and ditto for the speakers.

Above all, you can get out there, yourself, and speak whenever and wherever possible to a variety of audiences and groups. Here are some suggested places where you could speak, and most, or all, of these organizations would be delighted:

- Civic clubs
- Schools and colleges
- A wide variety of associations
- Historical societies
- PTA meetings
- Health groups
- Hobby groups and clubs
- Fraternal organizations like Kiwanis, Rotary, Lion's clubs, Optimist, Elks, and others

- Patriotic organizations
- Political party functions
- Literary gatherings
- Worthy cause organizations
- Senior citizen groups
- International clubs

The above is just a partial list. There are other clubs, groups, organizations, and audiences that would welcome you as a speaker. In fact, if you developed enough skill as a speaker and truly perfected the ability to hold an audience via what you say and how you communicate it, you could receive fees for speaking and presenting programs for some audiences. Keep in mind that those organizations that pay their chosen speakers plan their programs far in advance. My point is that if you got good enough in front of an audience, you could definitely turn professional and earn money as a speaker. Many such speakers do very well financially and enjoy what they are doing.

To get that good, you would have to pull out all the stops. You would need to tape-record your talks and speeches and listen to them over and over, taking notes on how you could improve your voice, rate of speaking, variety, the use of strategic pauses, projecting more enthusiasm and sincerity into your presentation, and more. You would want also to videotape yourself giving a talk or speech and then critique yourself, noting what you do well and not so well. Speaking is like the guitar and other arts; there is usually room for more improvement.

You would have to upgrade your articulation to be sure you are pronouncing all the syllables of words and not running words and sentences together.

What I'm talking about here is the route, the road map, at least part of it, to becoming a champion public speaker. Would you be willing to pay the price to become this good in front of an audience? It would take dedication and time.

A good question you might ask is what is it that makes a

champion? There is something, a quality, beyond the traits most people exercise and apply daily to achieve a strong level of success. I call it the unknown factor, or X-plus. Some prefer to think of it as guidance or direction from the subconscious mind. Others simply call it "that certain something." There is no doubt, however, that the following characteristics are true of X-plus:

- X-plus is the something extra deep within a person that drives the individual to get ahead.

- X-plus makes one move out in front and go to the top of his or her job, profession, or vocation.

As you may have already guessed, X-plus is that unknown factor that causes a person to become a champion. Those who have it somehow know it, although they may call it something else.

As an example, take the case of George S. Patton. At the tender age of ten, Patton announced his intention to become a great soldier and general one day. From the time he chose his objective as a boy in California, he never wavered.

As a young cadet at West Point, the future general could have been dropped from the academy for failing math his first year. Patton instead went through the first tough year a second time, sparing no effort to earn rank and honors.

He attained his goal. In his relief of Bastogne, Belgium, the real end of Hitler's hopes during World War II, Patton's Third Army moved farther in less time, engaging more enemy divisions, than any other army in the history of the United States.

Patton would not yield and did not believe in giving up. His constant command was "attack, attack!" He knew even at the start of his amazing career that he could and would attain his goal. He fired his desire with a white heat to become a great general, and that is exactly what happened. Patton certainly drew from the reservoir of X-plus within him.

THE STUFF OF CHAMPIONS

Most of us fall by the wayside, especially if the going gets tough. Many persons who know they must address a group or speak to some audience wait until the last minute to prepare. The champion is not only prepared but eager to do well and has worked with the goal in mind. The champion reaches out for more; a champion is willing to keep trying to do better, to rise to greatness.

The spirit of a genius is stirring in the champion's soul, for the experts have proven that genius is largely the courage to keep trying, plus plain hard work.

Somehow, the X-plus quality enables many a budding champion to hear the sound of a distant drum. The roll is a call that says he or she can make it, even before he or she tries; it lets the champion know that he or she can and will make a unique mark in the world.

WHAT HOLDS AN AUDIENCE

Why do some speakers rivet the attention and interest of their audiences? There are a number of sound reasons including a compelling personality, strong ethics and credibility, meaning the speaker is well-prepared, honest, and has a topic right for the audience that he or she is about to address.

Holding an audience takes experience and an effective blend of all these tools. Eye-contact, life, enthusiasm, variety, sincerity, and all the rest combine in a truly dynamic speaker and one who has the ability to rivet an audience and keep them that way all the way through the speech.

Dynamic speakers like this give an audience more than they expected. Sometimes they even overwhelm an audience with such abilities that the presentations rise to the level or oratory.

Style, gusto, energy, and stirring the feelings of an audience make for an unforgettable speaker.

Now I ask you a question. How on earth can an average

speaker of today become this powerful behind the podium without practice? There is no other way other than being born with the natural gifts for it. Even in that case, a great deal of practice is still a must.

Just about everyone can upgrade their overall speaking ability if they are willing to practice. It sounds like harping, but it is true. A great and dynamic speaker may be within you and eager to give voice to many fine talks and speeches that could change the lives of audiences. Give that other you, that possible sleeping giant or champion behind the podium the opportunity to go the distance.

PART
IV

THE FOUR MAJOR SPEECHES

13

THE SPEECH TO INFORM

It often happens when different speakers stand before their audiences. They begin to speak, and it becomes very clear that their address has no objective or clear goal in mind. Remember the song titled "Rambling Rose?" In a very similar way, a speaker without an objective is off and rambling behind the podium.

In his excellent book, *The Process of Communication*, David Berlo states that "there's a real purpose in communicating; the words we can command, and the way we put them together affect what we think about, how we think, and whether we are thinking at all."

The point is clear. Every speech has a main objective, a basic purpose that the speaker has planned to achieve. Most speeches seek to fulfill one of the following four purposes:

1. To inform

2. To inspire

3. To entertain

4. To persuade

Now keep in mind that a given speech or talk may inform and also inspire. Speeches often cross borders in the sense they may persuade, entertain, and possibly inform listeners, but a speaker should have one major purpose such as to inform. This is the main overall goal, even though there may be elements of the others evident.

As a speaker, keep your eye then on the major target, which is one of the four purposes. Plan and present talks that attain mostly one key objective.

In Lincoln's "Gettysburg Address," the main purpose was clearly to inspire the audience, though there were elements in it that informed and persuaded as well:

> It is rather for us to be here dedicated to the great task remaining before us—that from these honored dead we take increased devotion to that cause for which they gave the last full measure of devotion—that we here highly resolve that these dead shall not have died in vain—that this nation, under God, shall have a new birth of freedom—and the government of the people, by the people, for the people, shall not perish from the earth.

Let's take a close look now at each of these four major kinds of speeches, for they are the backbone, the part and parcel, the key types that most talks focus on and seek to achieve.

THE SPEECH TO INFORM
To inform an audience means to teach them, to impart information to them so they will know or learn new material about the subject covered in this kind of speech.

To inform is also to clarify. You must clarify the facts or information which you have selected for your talk or speech.

To inform is to explain what something means, tell how a

certain process works, how an event took place, or the way in which something is used.

This is a very important type of speech. Audiences the world over gain new insight, ideas, and information on a huge variety of subjects via this kind of speech.

When you plan this speech, the thing to ask yourself is will the audience learn from your presentation? Again, the speech to inform should reflect this learning purpose or instructional purpose to a large degree.

Next, ask what is the best way to transmit this learning to your audience? Ask and develop the main points you need to get across, plus any sub-points, so your objective can be achieved.

Plan in advance what supporting materials you will use in this speech. Your choices are examples, quotations by experts, explanations, statistics, definitions, and others.

This planning and answers to questions about this speech will be a great help to you. Remember, your audience will hear your speech but once. You must strive to be well-prepared to fulfill your purpose for this speech, which is to inform your audience and help them to derive a genuine sense of having learned something about the subject.

Do not get too scientific or technical in this speech unless, of course, you are speaking to a group of technical people. Some statistics and details may naturally be necessary in certain speeches, but just don't go overboard with them.

Try your best to sum up what a mass of technical figures mean. Sum up their underlying meaning for your audience. Do advance work for your audience. They want to feel that you have done your homework as leader and interpreter of all facts and figures. Most of your listeners will want to follow you, but don't overload them with too many complicated points. If you do, they will take a mental holiday and tune out parts of your speech.

If possible, personalize your speech. Tie yourself and any related examples into the topic. This helps to hold and keep audience interest. The more you can relate the subject to your audience the more effective it will usually be, and never overestimate what the audience knows.

THE WORLD OF HOW-TO

Here is a valuable guideline that can help you a great deal whenever you present a speech to inform and get stuck for a worthy topic. Simply consider the enormous world of the how-to, meaning how-to do all manner of things—study better, make more money, plan more fun vacations, raft on the Colorado River, develop the art of management, cross Canada by auto, or whatever.

The point here is that the world of how-to, covering all manner of subjects, gives you access to hundreds and probably thousands of possible subjects for a speech to inform or address, or shorter talk with the basic purpose of informing your audience.

With the world of how-to ready for you to brainstorm for the best subjects for you, you should never have any trouble finding a good subject for this kind of speech.

Where else are clusters of subjects waiting for you for a speech to inform? How about speeches about events, about new ideas (that have come along in almost every field), speeches about processes in which you tell how something works, speeches about mere objects (such as magazines, baseball cards, the U.S. Navy, Canadian trains, Big Ben in London, golf balls, and hundreds of other things.

Don't overlook another possibility for this popular speech to inform. Consider presenting your talk or speech about a person. He or she might be an outstanding athlete, a business person on today's cutting edge, a foreign policy expert, authority on traveling with a circus, a military officer, teacher, celebrity, musician, film star, or whoever. Speeches to inform can be and are about fascinating, unique, or interesting people.

SPEECH TO INFORM TITLE EXAMPLES

To give you still more examples of this major kind of talk, take a look at the following titles of actual speeches that have been presented to audiences:

"New Year's Resolutions I Wish I Could Keep"
"Planning Where You'll Be in 2020 and Beyond"
"How to Cope With Job Burnout"
"Have We Seen the Last of El Nino?"
"The Most Famous Choir in the World"
"I Stood Where Becket Was Assassinated"
"The Incredible Predictions of Nostradamus"

EXAMPLE OF A SPEECH TO INFORM

What follows is an example of the speech to inform in action. The first part of the speech only is given, and you will notice that this address was presented for a high school audience or assembly group.

Finding Your Right Work Field

High school days are wonderful times, but they go by faster than most people realize. If you haven't already done so, now is the time to be zeroing in on what you honestly feel is the right vocation for you.

Do not wait until you have graduated, are working, or through your first years in college. Wise up to that ticking clock on the wall. Now is the time to start looking for clues that point to the right field for you.

Know first that there is indeed a right field or vocation for you, but you've got to do some serious thinking about yourself and your interests, in order to find where you belong. Maybe you think you are still too young to follow the age-old advice to "know thyself." It's your life and work. You will save a lot of frustration, wasted years, and energy if you can make a right choice today about your future.

Ask this question of yourself today, tomorrow, and every day. Where do you belong?

In what field of work can you make a strong contribution and also be happy? These are critical questions you need to answer. The first step in narrowing down the job-vocation field is to sit down and make a list of all your interest areas.

Write down the various fields of work that have interested you in the past or interest you today. Your list might include seven or more areas. Your next step is to decide in your mind which fields interest you the most. Rank them number one, two, and three in order of their degree of interest to you.

After you have chosen three major fields of interest, the next thing to do is to read up on these three vocations or job fields. You already have some knowledge about them, no doubt, or you would not be interested in them at present. The idea now is to learn more about all three. Say, for example, that you listed newspaper reporter, engineer, and sales rep. Then these three would be studied, in order to gain more information about them.

There are some excellent ways to get current information about most fields of interest to you. Write to the companies that are directly engaged in the lines of work that are of interest to you. Ask them for any material they can send you about the field, how to get into it, special training or qualifications needed, and other questions you may have.

The above speech went on to make library exploration suggestions, research via the Internet and electronic sources, plus personal interviews of people in the fields of interest.

I have given this speech to high school and youth groups and it has been favorably received. Did you notice the strong "how-to" nature of the speech? Again, the speech to inform imparts information, teaches, explains a process or how to do something (in this case obtain helpful information about making a vocation decision).

Remember, the speech to inform is one of the most helpful and popular kinds of speeches. It helps to keep countries developing, communicates valuable and useful information in thousands of subject areas, and continues to change, improve, or upgrade the lives of audiences.

Whenever you plan a talk, address, or speech to inform, turn to this section and read it over again as you plan and practice your speech.

Always keep in mind that if your talk helps just one listener in your audience, it has been successful. It is far more likely to have an impact on a number of listeners in your audiences. That is one of the real powers of spoken communication. Develop skill for the speech to inform and learn how to get your material across to audiences, and you can and will change lives for the better and make a worthy contribution as a speaker. You may well decide to specialize in this kind of informative talk. More power to you, the power to inform audiences.

14 _____

THE SPEECH TO INSPIRE

What does it mean to inspire an audience? This is another purpose or reason for speaking to an audience. In this special kind of speech, your goal is to uplift the audience or to place a spotlight on the subject to the point that it is ennobled.

Inspiration may have any of the following effects on listeners (or a combination of them):

• This listener feels "on fire" about your speech or elements in it.

• The listener feels an influence to achieve something or perhaps to make his or her life count more. A change in the listener's basic attitude takes place.

• The listener may feel that "all is not lost," "life can be and often is beautiful," "the best is yet to be" or whatever.

• An idea, viewpoint, subject, or theory is cast in such a light, or communicated in such an ennobled way by you, the speaker, that the listener comes away with a fresh, vivid, and possibly exciting new perspective.

YOU, AS SPEAKER, MUST BE INSPIRED

The key to doing well with the speech to inspire is to be inspired yourself, regarding your chosen subject. If you are inspired as the communicator, it is much more likely that your audience will be too as they listen to you.

Napoleon Hill, the illustrious speaker and author, once opened his speech with these words, which assured his audience that he was an inspired speaker:

"I have always tried to make each speech better than the last one before. Tonight is no exception. This will be the greatest lecture I've ever given in my life."

HOW TO BE AN INSPIRED SPEAKER

First, speak from the heart. This kind of communication is powerful and definitely inspires listeners.

Try to stir your listeners to the very core of their beings. In other words, move them in such a way by your speech that they will be different people from that point forward.

Believe in your material, the subject and plan of your speech, so much that it will come across to your audience. Get excited about what you're communicating.

Try to build your talk or speech to a high point of maximum interest. If you can do this, you will be more likely to keep the maximum attention of your audience.

Use the power of your individual personality to make your material inspiring. A speaker's compelling personality can wring a lot of inspiration out of the spoken word. Make them remember you in the weeks and months ahead, not just the ABC's of your speech material. Do your best to make them think of you for some time to come as a truly dynamic speaker.

STRONG EXAMPLES AND ANECDOTES CAN BUILD INSPIRATION

Powerful and unforgettable examples and anecdotes (little stories with a point) are a must in this speech and do much to build inspiration.

In a speech I have given a number of times for various audiences, I wanted my listeners to realize how easy today's modern era is compared with the colonial period. I decided to compare or contrast the two time periods with an example, and here is an excerpt from the one I used:

> An old Italian proverb says that "he conquers who endures." The early colonists were victorious over their obstacles because they would not give up. Crossing the ocean in small inadequate boats was no little feat in itself. Many wondered if they would even get to the new land alive. And when they did, the struggle for survival really began. Indian threat, famine, malaria, unfit drinking water, swamps, and having to hunt for food were only a few of their problems. The need to build a fort for protection from the Indians was imperative. To top it all, ships bringing much needed supplies from England got lost or seldom got through. Despite the overwhelming difficulties, a scant hundred years later, colonists in Williamsburg, Virginia, had come amazingly far.

Examples, also often called illustrations, help a great deal to clarify what is being said, make a point, and above all make it more interesting.

Here is another example that I have used in a number of talks where my purpose was to inspire the audience:

While a semi-invalid, Robert Louis Stevenson completed thirty thousand words of Dr. Jekyll and Mister Hyde. When his wife criticized it, after he read it to her, Stevenson became enraged and threw the manuscript into the fire, saying she was right about it. He promptly returned to his bed with pencil and fresh paper. He wrote three more days with little sleep and emerged with a completely new manuscript of the same idea. The slender 149-page book, The Strange Case of Dr. Jekyll and Mister Hyde, as published in 1886 for one shilling. When the London Times praised the new book, it quickly became a best seller, selling 40,000 copies in six months.

SPEECH TO INSPIRE TITLE EXAMPLES

Here are some suggestions for a speech to inspire. You can come up with more ideas by searching your own past experiences, training, education, travels, jobs, and adventures. Research your memory well when you are planning this kind of speech. You should also watch a variety of publications for possible ideas and examples you can use. The same is true for the Internet, electronic sources, books, newsletters, and whatever. Your friends, relatives, neighbors, and family members are often a good source for speech or talk ideas and anecdotes.

Here are some speech to inspire title examples:

1. "You Were Born to Be a Champion" (to inspire listeners to go for the roses, be more successful, and achieve more in life).

2. "If You Can Read, You're Rich" (to inspire listeners

to appreciate the rewards of reading and to actually read more).

3. "The First Woman President of the United States" (to inspire listeners that the nation has reached the right time for this first in its history).

4. "The Splendor of England and Scotland" (to inspire listeners to visit and travel in both areas).

5. "The Most Inspiring Person I Have Known" (this can suggest one or more persons who have had a strong influence in your life. Remember always that a speech to inspire can be about an individual.

HOW TO TELL IF YOU'RE
REALLY INSPIRING THEM

There are some definite ways you can tell if your speech to inspire is going over well or not. Here are some clues or signs to watch for. They reveal if you are accomplishing your purpose to inspire:

• Several or more in your audience are not paying attention, whispering to each other, looking around the room, or obviously not with you.

• Some in your audience appear to be visibly moved. Some speeches are planned and presented so well that they really get through to listeners and truly inspire them.

• The audience before you is sitting there like they are spellbound. Most of them appear to be closely following what you are saying.

EXAMPLE OF A SPEECH TO INSPIRE

Here is the opening, and some excerpts, of a speech to inspire. Please take note that when this speech was presented, the "sleeping soldier" still lay at Arlington. He is no longer there, since the body was identified and then buried in his home state: (I presented this speech on Veterans Day.)

The Sleeping Soldier at Arlington

In honored glory, there beneath the sod, there lies an unknown soldier—know but to God.

Whoever said the public has a short memory uttered a profound truth. Now well over a half century since World War II, Americans have generally forgotten the sacrifices of thousands of young Americans, who gave their limbs, blood, and lives that we might live in continued freedom.

The lives of those young soldiers, sailors, and pilots were just as precious as those who fought in Korea, Vietnam, and Desert Storm. We owe an enormous debt to all those courageous American fighting men and women who took on the burden of the second world war.

Regardless of which war, or how many years between wars, those who face hell itself in any and every war must never be forgotten. "He loves his country best who strives to make it best," said Robert Ingersoll, American lawyer. Every person who risks his or her own life daily for his country does love his country best, for by his or her presence on each foreign war scene, or in the air, or on the sea, he fights to keep his country free. That is patriotism.

The end of the speech went like this:

As you go about your life and work in this still the greatest land on earth, remember the heritage passed on to you by America's fallen men at arms. Stand up for her, as they did. Never forget the sleeping soldier, the unknown solider, at Arlington and all he represents—America at her best.

15

THE SPEECH TO ENTERTAIN

Many think of the speech to entertain as the most popular, and it is the favorite to listen to for many. This type of talk or speech can do much to brighten up the lives of audiences. To entertain is to bring pleasure to others. It's a worthy goal.

This type of speech used to be called the after dinner speech. It has long been traditional to expect any after dinner speaker to be an entertaining one, though this does not always turn out to be the case.

When clubs, associations, and other groups of people gather to have their meetings, with or without dinner, they then have a speaker lined up to entertain them. Such speeches may be presented in large hotel ballrooms or formal meeting and assembly rooms.

The speech to entertain may also inform and inspire and perhaps persuade to one degree or another. Certainly elements of the other major speeches may well be present, even though the overall purpose and objective is to entertain.

A lot of dinner programs take the time to introduce guests of honor and others at the banquet table and attend to various business matters of the group or organization, before the main speaker is introduced. Other programs go right to the speaker as soon as dinner is over. By its very nature, the after dinner speech implies something light and entertaining.

PICK AN ENTERTAINING SUBJECT

You certainly want to avoid any dull, lifeless, boring, or uninteresting subjects for this kind of speech. Look for a subject with the following qualities:

* Amusing
* Light and sparkling (avoid heavy subjects)
* Attractive
* Entertainment appeal
* Strong degree of interest

Just about every audience, large or small, has bored people in it. Who knows what kind of day or week they may have had? Some of them may be in the middle of serious problems or facing them soon in their lives. There they are, sitting there looking at you and waiting to hear your talk.

Your job is to make them feel amused and to try and entertain them. Perhaps you can make them laugh a bit (you do not have to) and go back to their lives feeling a little happier, a bit lighter, and generally better for having heard your presentation.

The essential goal you are after in this particular speech is to amuse the audience. This does not mean that you have failed if your listeners do not laugh a lot and almost roll in the aisles. An audience, or many of them, may be amused without a single laugh being heard from them.

In a real sense, subjects that offer escape often work well. Through your choice of a subject and your presentation it's very possible to take your listeners on a journey. Speakers who present travel programs on exotic lands or glamorous cities are a good example of this escapism benefit. Such travel programs entertain and amuse audiences while also informing them.

USING HUMOR IN THE SPEECH TO ENTERTAIN

Some humor will add strength to this type of speech, though

please realize that your presentation does not have to be filled with jokes, witty lines, and cracker-barrel humor. Many talks and speeches entertain without relying on a series of jokes. The thing to shoot for is an overall amusing effect. There may be only a few places in your talk or speech that bring an occasional laugh, but if the total effect of your material is amusing, then you have succeeded and entertained your audience.

One standard definition of humor is "a comic quality causing amusement—the humor of a situation." Another basic definition states that "humor is the faculty of perceiving what is amusing or comical."

Take a look at the following humor bits and their sources:

"Have you heard about my million dollar movie offer? If I pay a million dollars, they'll let me be in a movie." (TV weatherman.)

"If I die, find my wife at Wal-Mart." (A frustrated husband.)

"What this country needs is a cheaper place to park." (Humorist.)

"Sex is here to stray." (A Bob Hope one-liner.)

PLUS BENEFITS OF HUMOR

Laughter is an antidote for the day-to-day frustrations that can destroy a healthy person as surely as some great tragedy.

A sense of humor lifts the emotional strain in which you may hold yourself. It casts out gloomy thoughts. Humor helps you to relax. It changes saggy facial muscles and saddened eyes, turning them into a refreshing smile. Humor transforms a dull routine and provides a counterbalance, which is needed in an age of work and worry.

SPECIFICS ON LAUGHTER

Studies show that laughter stimulates the human brain to produce hormones called datecholamines. These hormones decrease arthritis pain and relieve serious allergy, plus other problems. Consider the following specifics:

• Laughter helps your entire respiratory system by cleaning it out.

• When you laugh your heart, thorax, abdomen, diaphragm, and lungs are exercised.

• Laughter increases your heart rate and overall circulation.

• Laughter keeps you well and for longer periods of time.

• Uproarious laughter, the really crack-your-ribs kind, gives the muscles in your arms, legs, and face a workout.

HUMOR IS MANY THINGS

Humor is often the ability to take the familiar and make it seem funny. Professional comics and television talk show hosts have a talent for turning the familiar into something funny.

Humor is the fine art of exaggeration. Listen carefully to entertaining speakers, comics, and amusing persons on television, and you will see how much they exaggerate in their humor techniques.

Humor can be satire, a play on words, or sarcasm. It may be association with something else (often unexpected), understatement, and just plain surprise.

Humor may also be irony, which is saying a thing in such a way that the opposite is obviously intended.

PREPARING FOR A SPEECH
TO ENTERTAIN

Whenever you plan to present a speech to entertain, the smart thing to do early on is to get more humor and laughter into your life. Here are some proven steps for developing a stronger sense of humor:

1. Think about humor more and what is funny or amusing. This step alone can trigger a variety of amusing subjects for entertaining talks.

2. Experiment in taking something known and familiar and then making it seem funny. To do this, use the tools of association, understatement, and surprise. Use exaggeration too. Satire, sarcasm, plays on words, parody, and burlesque are all sources of humor and offer tips for making something in your speech funny.

3. Stay alert to the sources of humor all around you in books, newspapers, magazines, newsletters, on the Internet, radio, television, in cartoons, comic strips, greeting cards, various software programs for computers, and just about everywhere that human beings live and work.

4. Keep an ongoing humor notebook in which you write down the funny ideas, humorous bits you discover, and amusing subjects or titles for talks and speeches. This is an excellent way to train your mind to spot humor and be alert for it.

5. Be especially alert for humorous signs. There are lots of them out there wherever you live or travel including overseas. Watch for these amusing signs. Here are just a few of many such amusing signs spotted in various places:

- "No shirts, no shoes, no service" (Sign in a Kentucky restaurant.)
- "Be careful driving. Chicago is full of Oldsmobiles and Cadillacs." (Sign seen at the city limits.)
- "You don't have to be a stripper to drop your clothes here." (Sign in a Los Angeles cleaners.)
- "Fight pollution. Ride a horse." (Bumper sticker on car.)

PRESENTING THE SPEECH TO ENTERTAIN

Here are some time-tested ways for creating an amusing effect in this kind of speech. You have a number of choices:

1. Open your speech with an unusual remark.

2. Relate an amusing story or anecdote.

3. Refer to a humorous experience you recently had.

4. Try to end your speech on an amusing point. Skip any detailed summation for this speech. Use something, preferably funny, which ties in or condenses your main points in a nutshell.

In most cases, the speech to entertain goes better with a brisk pace. Don't rush through it talking at too fast a rate, but the pace should be a bit more swift than other types of speeches. Try to achieve the following whenever you give this type of talk or speech:
- Be cheerful and good-natured.
- Be optimistic and positive.
- Try to sound friendly and like a good-humored person.
- Act like you are truly enjoying yourself and like you are glad to be there speaking to your audience.

You will need crisp and memorable examples and anecdotes (little stories) for this kind of speech. Some likely sources for useful examples include your own recent amusing experiences, other entertaining things that have happened to you, interesting material from the lives of others you know, family adventures perhaps, something you hear on television, or see on the Internet and maybe in a comic strip. There is a variety of sources for amusing material.

Remember that this kind of talk or amusing speech needs a structure, a framework, just as the others do. This means you must plan and practice an effective introduction, middle, and conclusion for your speech. You will want a strong beginning and definite way to grab audience attention. Your audience will decide from your opening if they want to keep listening to you.

Deal with the main points in the body or middle of your talk or speech as simply as possible. In fact, you should choose very clear points, leading up to each one with an attractive example or story.

Do not use all your best material in the early part of your speech. Save some of the most amusing bits for the latter part and ending of your speech.

SPEECH TO ENTERTAIN TITLE EXAMPLES

Here are some actual speeches to entertain that have been presented to a variety of audiences. Again, your own life, experience, and background offer you an excellent source for possible subjects:

"Kids Say the Funniest Things"

"Their Names Were Magic" (A speech on some of the memorable stars, actors, singers, comedians, and entertainers.)

"How to Become a Circus Clown"

"Applause Is What Performers Live for"

Why I Would Rather Drop Than Shop"

Remember, the trouble with most of us is that we're about 50 laughs behind. It may be an old cliché, but "laugh and the world laughs with you" is still good advice. Learn to laugh at yourself first and then at the many funny things about life and the world, and you will always have a good source of subjects for a speech to entertain.

There is humor all around you everyday, if you will learn to spot it, collect it, appreciate it, and share it with others in speeches that amuse and entertain.

Laughter and humor are part and parcel of what makes life worth living. Humor is a magic elixir that will enrich your life as a speaker and in many other ways. Start enjoying more of it at once. You'll be glad you did.

EXAMPLE OF A SPEECH TO ENTERTAIN
The main purpose of the following speech was to entertain the audience, but it also informed and contained elements of inspiration. The introduction of the speech and excerpts from it went like this:

In Search of Adventure and Travel
Shades of James Bond! The itch for adventure is taking many persons all over the world by storm. It's a fever, the adventure fever, and it's hitting a lot of people where they live. It may have invaded your life.

It has no doubt invaded your life in one way or another. Someone you know has probably responded to the lure of adventure and travel in one way or at some time. Maybe someone where you work just up and quit his or her job and took off to grow bananas in South America or whatever.

A friend of mine in the Midsouth area has been busting to see Alaska for years. He's had a yen to explore this last frontier for some time. He held back and tried to resist the call, while hoping to find someone to make the trip with him. Finally, he could wait no longer. He left last spring for points north, and I'm afraid the lower 49 may have lost him to Alaska for sometime to come, perhaps even for good.

The point is that it's what he wanted to do. Nobody held a gun to his head. He had the itch to flee to Alaska—and what he calls the Yukon good life—for years. The itch to cut loose just grew too strong. He left a good job as an investment counselor and a girl who thought she was going to be his bride this year. As it turned out, he hitched up with Alaska instead.

Adventure fever is contagious. There is no doubt about it. You can't pick up a newspaper or magazine without reading at least one or more true accounts of someone somewhere who has severed the home town connection, job responsibility, and maybe even family ties to take off out there somewhere to do his or her own thing.

Englishman John Merrill, an author of books about the countryside and a man in love with long distance walking, spent some ten months walking around the coastline of England, Wales, and Scotland. His remarkable seven thousand mile adventure consumed, required, wore out, or used up the following items:

- Three pairs of boots
- Hundreds of gallons of milk
- 33-pairs of socks
- 1,000 bars of chocolate
- 60-pounds of equipment

Merrill met hundreds of people on his walk and was interviewed by the local press and radio/television along the way. He began walking promptly at eight-thirty each morning and quit for the day at five. He was invited to a number of evening events as he made the marathon journey.

Merrill's adventure itch not only resulted in his personal enjoyment of seeing the changing coastline; he put the story of his adventurous walk, the events of it, the hardships, and total experience into a book—along with maps, photos, and material in the back describing the equipment he used.

His book, *Turn Right At Lands End* (Oxford Illustrated Press), has lined up a second marathon for Merrill—this time a long tour of speaking dates to lecture all over England, Scotland, and Wales about his walk to end all walks.

Now whenever others with the itch for adventure nudging their innards read about Merrill's amazing adventure, you can see their eyes light up and their chins drop as they drool about the idea of cutting loose on an adventure of their own: "God, if I could only do something like that myself," they say.

What fans the contagious spirit of adventure is this hearing or reading about how someone actually did it—someone who had the daring, imagination, and guts to make an adventurous idea in their minds become a reality.

What else adds to this desire for adventure that has no doubt suggested itself to you at one time or another? Wilderness movies show people living out in the far distant woods or building a winter home in the mountains. These films chalk up a large gross at the box-office because it's really what a lot of people would like to do—to get-away-from-it-all and live off the land, starting a new life in a vastly different surrounding.

Why is this desire to get away there? Maybe because millions do not feel they can cope with the mind-boggling problems of modern life that sometimes engulf them. They want to escape or at least many do. They like the idea and promise of a fresh start somewhere else. The world looks like it's rushing to the cliff-top at times. There are wars or rumors of wars, trouble raising youngsters these days, sudden drops in the stock market, and all the rest. The years also just keep on rushing by.

Those with an adventurous bent or spirit simply reason that if they are going to do the one or more things they have always wanted to—if they are going to make that adventure they long for in their hearts come true—they had better get at it before everything goes off the deep end. This is at least the way many people reason.

It is really the times we live in then that lend support to the contagious fever of adventure. Have you experienced this fever? Then welcome to the club. Adventure films, talks, ads, and commercials fuel this itch for adventure. You might well say that many who are sensitive to this contagious craving for adventure have blood in their adventure streams.

The speech went on to describe some of my own adventure trips to London, Paris, Colorado, the west coast, Ireland, Scotland, and other places. It also told of my great adventure crossing Canada by train and discovering the beauty and wide spaces of that fascinating land.

The speech was well-received and hopefully kindled many adventurous trips by listeners in my audience.

16

THE SPEECH TO PERSUADE

The ability to persuade via the spoken word is real power. The art of persuasion is one of the true marvels of life. It keeps nations moving forward, cities growing, and human lives achieving. Take away persuasion and thousands of products and services would stop being sold. In addressing an audience, the speech to persuade is one of the most important of them all.

As a strong example, take the world of advertising. The lights burn late on Madison Avenue, in New York, where ad people are crafting new commercials and headlines designed to grab your attention and make you buy certain products and services.

Look at the mail order pitches you receive every week. What is it but persuasion? They even resort to all manner of gimmicks and techniques meant to get you to open their envelopes. Many of these envelopes received have what looks like a check inside made out to you—but of course it's only an enticement to open the letter. They must get you to open the envelope and read their pitch or they're dead in the water and they know it.

Where else does persuasion go on in daily life? How about the courtrooms of any country? Lawyers give their summaries before juries about to make important decisions. Drop in to most courtrooms as a visitor, and you will hear many strong examples of persuasion in action.

Today you see a growing number of persuasive communications on the Internet, and there will be more and more as new millions come on line.

The military branches must continue to persuade, in order to meet their new recruit demands from year to year. New techniques of marketing and persuasion are continually studied by military officials in order to stay competitive and get the newcomers they need.

You go to a trade show or fair and see persuasion in action. The attendant calls for your attention and does his best to get you to stop at his certain booth or buy his product. It's all persuasion.

We briefly mentioned the army of salespeople who move the goods and services of their nations. They are on the front lines of persuasive communication, for they get the prospects for a thousand products and services to sign on the dotted line, reach for their credit cards or checkbooks, and buy. If salespeople suddenly stopped doing their thing, via skillful and creative persuasion, the economy of nations would grind to a much slower pace or even come to a halt.

Candidates for president and other offices rise or fall, depending on their basic ability to persuade people to vote for them.

Many fine speakers have made effective use of persuasive communication via the spoken word. In so doing, they lifted the horizons of mankind and made the world a better place.

Never forget this vital truth about oral persuasion: It has the potential power to sway the masses. The gift of oratory is an awesome one, when developed enough, and used with intelligence and wisdom by those who have the skill.

THE WORDS OF ARISTOTLE

Keep in mind the words and guidance of the great Aristotle: "The use of a persuasive speech is to lead to decisions."

The belief and conviction of some members of an audience are rather easy to change by a skilled speaker. Others in every audience may be much more difficult to sway. To persuade those holding mildly held beliefs, you simply need to have a solid number of logical and sound reasons why the listeners should change their opinions.

When the beliefs of an audience are very strong ones, you will need all the persuasive power you can bring to bear on the subject. This means evidence, and lots of it, in the form of facts, statements and quotes by noted experts or authorities in the field, strong examples, illustrations, statistics, and all the back-up, supporting ammunition you can muster.

AUDIENCE IDENTIFICATION

When planning your speech to persuade, it's a good idea to decide exactly what you seek to persuade your audience about. Then determine in advance how you intend to go about achieving it.

Ask yourself how your audience can be persuaded. What kinds of evidence will be the most useful to you? This type of speech takes careful planning and outlining. One of the first things you must decide in this type of talk is how to get the audience to not only accept you, as a speaker, but also to believe what you say or communicate.

You need then to win over your audience soon, and the best way to do it is through some kind of identification. When planning and outlining your speech to persuade, ask yourself these questions:

1. How can I identify myself with my audience? There are clues for doing this in the background, interests,

and common goals which you share with your
audience.

2. What appeals or motivating influences can you cite, in
   order to reach your audience (such as patriotism or
   family and home appeals, religious, or political
   appeals)?

HOW TO IDENTIFY WITH YOUR AUDIENCE

Take a look at the following ways the speaker chose to
identify with the audience, which no doubt helped to gain and
keep their attention:

Speaker: "While this is my first opportunity to visit in England, I have long been concerned about the well-being and future
of your nation."

Speaker: "The American way of life, as we know and love
it, is threatened today."

Speaker: "I grew up in this state and still think of it as my
second home."

OUTLINING YOUR SPEECH TO PERSUADE

The following steps will result in an effective and persuasive talk or speech, assuming that you can present or communicate the material in a forceful and compelling way:

1. Write out a clear basic sentence stating exactly what it
   is you will be asking the audience to do. What is it
   you want to persuade them to do (support a cause,
   cast a vote, change an opinion, stop smoking, set more
   goals, invest in the stock market, try their hand at a
   new business, understand a different view, or perhaps
   to take action on some matter)?

2. Decide on your introduction for the speech. You need an especially strong opening or hook in order to grab attention. An appealing title will help.

3. Determine and collect the strongest evidence you can obtain for backing up the reasons why your audience should make a change in their attitude, opinion, or whatever. Know your evidence well and know where you will use it in your speech. (Use many examples, testimony, quotes, comparisons, facts, statistics, and illustrations.)

4. Find a way to identify with your audience so they will tend to accept and believe what you say.

5. Write out your introduction.

6. Plan and write out the main points to be covered in the middle (body) of your talk or speech.

7. Plan and write out the conclusion. Remember, you can summarize your main points, use a strong story, example, or illustration that wraps up the gist of your speech or ties it all together, or just brings it to a logical ending.

TIPS TO KEEP YOUR PERSUASIVE SPEECH ON TARGET

Aristotle said that the only essential parts of a speech are:

1. The statements

2. The argument

Generally speaking, a forceful style of delivery by you, as the speaker, can help persuade your audience. Persuasion is more difficult to achieve than informing, entertaining, or inspiring an audience. I especially urge you to tape-record your speech (or videotape it), and perhaps others you present, and then listen to it, or view it and listen, making specific notes on how you can improve the overall effect of your speech. Aristotle emphasized that strong and effective persuasion must do three things:

- Work on the emotions of the audience
- Give the right impression of the speaker's character
- Prove the truth of the statements made.

Never lose sight of your objective in this speech, which is to persuade the audience to accept what you are saying, and believe it, thus possibly changing either a mildly or stubbornly held view or opinion. Or your goal may be to lead the audience to take some form of action.

Your style of delivery, use of clear words, skillful blending of short and long sentences, the overall way you handle all the material of your speech, your choice and use of motivating appeals, how well you succeed in exciting the listener's emotions, and repetition of important facts or evidence will all determine whether or not real persuasion takes place.

SPEECH TO PERSUADE TITLE EXAMPLES

In case you are stumped for a Speech to Persuade idea, here are some suggestions for this type of talk. Most of them are meant to stimulate the audience to action or to change or enforce a belief or opinion held by the audience:

"Children Are Children for Just a Little While" (To persuade the audience to make the most of their short time and chance to influence children.)

"Teaching Deserves Your Best" (To persuade an audience of mostly teachers to give only their best to the profession. This speech, you will note, would also have elements of inspiration.)

"Your Vote Can Make a Difference" (To persuade the audience that their vote is very important and should be exercised.)

"Tobacco Companies Are to Blame (Are Not to Blame) for Deaths From Smoking" (To persuade the audience on either side of this topic—that tobacco companies are responsible or that they are not to blame.) NOTE: A persuasive case could be made for either side of this topic.

"Your Brain Improves With Use" (To persuade the audience to support and take an active part in continuing education—plus the truth that most humans use only one-third, or less, of their brain power.

"UFOs Are for Real" (To persuade the audience why they should believe in UFOs.)

"If You Can Read, You're Rich" (To persuade the audience to read more and communicate the joys and plus benefits of reading more.)

EXAMPLE OF A SPEECH TO PERSUADE

I have presented the following speech to persuade a number of times. It is based on the code or principles for becoming more successful recommended by that illustrious promoter P.T. Barnum.

You will note that this speech (parts and excerpts from it) also informs, inspires, and entertains. It's a good example of a speech that crosses borders. My main purpose in presenting it was to persuade my audience that each one of them could become a more successful person by following these guidelines. Barnum's code for success is very persuasive on its own, and it certainly worked well for him and made him very successful. Some of the principles could be combined, in order to reduce the number of main points presented.

Be sure to note the examples, anecdotes, and quotes from Barnum, himself, which form the supporting materials for the speech. This proved to be a most successful persuasive speech for me, and audiences have responded to it warmly.

You Can Become More Successful

P.T. Barnum was known as the greatest American showman of his day. When he died in 1891, the *London Times* called him "that fine flower of western civilization, that arbiter elegantiarum to Demos, who gave a luster to America. His name is a proverb already, and proverb it will continue."

Barnum left what he personally felt was a surefire way a person could become more successful. He believed that if one would follow the rules he discovered and practiced himself, that person would achieve substantial success in his or her chosen work and in life.

At the young age of nineteen, Barnum founded and edited a newspaper in Danbury, Connecticut. This personal effort enabled him to show his interest in politics, and his *Herald of Freedom* newspaper brought him to public notice. Throughout his life, Barnum often wrote for syndicates and magazines on various subjects. Much of his time was also spent speaking to audiences, his main lecture being "The Art of Money-Getting."

In 1844, Barnum toured England and Europe. He brought the famous Jenny Lind, the "Swedish nightingale," to America in 1850. Largely through his skillful promotion, Jenny became a front page celebrity who grossed nearly a million dollars at the nations's box offices. That was quite a huge fortune in those days. Offered the Democratic nomination for governor of Connecticut, in 1852, Barnum declined but later ran for Congress, though he was defeated. In the 1870s, he opened his "Greatest Show on Earth" in Brooklyn and enjoyed great success with it. His museum, menagerie, and circus required some five-hundred men and horses for transporting.

Barnum's circus later merged with that of J.A. Bailey to form the Barnum and Bailey Circus. Barnum used an imported elephant named Jumbo for his show. He seemed to have a sixth sense for knowing what audiences would enjoy.

Called the "Magician of Mirth," "The Lord of Laughter and Fun," "The Dispenser of Amusement," and "The Prince of Humbugs," P.T. Barnum loved his popularity. He followed a very strict idea or rule book of showmanship, always giving the public more than it paid for and keeping his shows free from all indecencies.

Barnum thought that the common man deserved amusement for his spare time—entertainment that was wholesome and non-corrupting. Known as the father of modern day publicity, he created the popular museum and turned tent carnivals into the modern three-ring circus.

The illustrious showman did a lot of work for the city of Bridgeport, Connecticut. Its beautiful Seaside Park was a gift from Barnum. He also laid out many streets of the main city and planted seventeen thousand trees. A beautiful fountain was placed in a park in front of a church. Eventually, he owned more than three hundred buildings.

Barnum often said he couldn't live in a town without trying to improve it. He served as mayor of Bridgeport, where he was born, from 1875 to 1876. Barnum was sunny and alive at all times, with an inborn desire to make people happy. He went to great lengths to thrill children and often fixed the prices and days to be more convenient for them. No matter where he went, he always had a cheerful word for everyone. His presence at one of his shows was enough to usually greatly increase the box office take.

A showman to the end, Barnum's last words when he died in Philadelphia were a request to know the day's receipts of the circus. In 1907, his circus was sold to the Ringling Brothers.

Great success that he was, Barnum followed his own code book of rules. He often passed these principles along to others who sought to be more successful. Do not underestimate the importance of these sound principles that are still just as valid and useful today as they were in Barnum's era. Here is Barnum's master list of action steps that can make you much more successful:

1. Select the vocation which is most congenial to your tastes.

Millions have to literally drag themselves to work each day because they made a wrong vocational choice. Take stock of your situation. If you're in the wrong kind of work or career, start making plans now to leave it as soon as you can for work more to your liking. Life goes by fast enough anyway. You might just as well be doing work you are suited for and like.

2. Exercise both caution and boldness. Before rush-

ing into some project, try to determine your chances of success. Too much caution is of course dangerous, and the same is true of too much boldness. While exercising both caution and boldness, depend on your own personal exertions. Students who earn academic degrees learn this fortunately at a fairly early age. They know they have to stay in there and keep plugging away at the books to get their degrees.

Trusting and depending on your own personal efforts can pay off in better jobs, advanced degrees, more money, and all kinds of personal accomplishment.

3. Learn something useful to fall back on, if things do not go the way you hope and plan.

Having worked as a grocery store clerk after grammar school, the first thing Barnum did after moving to New York, in 1834, was to open such a store. Eight years later, when a New York museum went on sale, Barnum managed to open it as his own Barnum's American Museum.

Barnum's promotional abilities and knowledge paid off for the rest of his life, but his grocery clerk experience was always something he could fall back on if necessary. This is still a very sound course of action for the dawn and early on decades of a new century and very likely for the entire 21st century.

4. Whatever you do, do it with all your might. If you have to, work at your goal or objective both early and late. Put your whole self into it.

Perhaps the best way to think of this idea of commanding all your might and powers is to view it as determination. A determined person is a powerful individual.

Boxing immortal Jim Corbett was determined to defeat the great John L. Sullivan in the historic fight held in New Orleans on September 7, 1892. The purse was for $25,000 (a great deal of money then), but Corbett was so sure he would win that he also placed a side bet on himself for $10,000. When the bell sounded, Corbett began to dodge Sullivan and kept on doing it. Quickly sidestepping the champion, Corbett broke Sullivan's nose. Sullivan roared, "Come in and fight!" Corbett refused. For twenty rounds this continued, until Corbett realized that Sullivan was ripe for the kill. Corbett's main strategy was simply to avoid Sullivan's rushes with style, while continually getting in counter punches. Corbett knocked the champion out in twenty-one rounds.

Corbett held the title for the next four years, and his victory made him a man of international importance overnight. His advice for more successful and happier living is worth remembering and following: "When you're weary from trying, don't quit; fight one more round. That one more round may make all the difference and bring you success."

It should also be said that it usually takes a determined person to fight one more round, go the distance, and attain an objective or goal.

5. Don't let the horror of the blues or depression take over you.

Barnum advised everyone to fight back. Fight the blues with all your might, for depression and the blues can wreck your plans and wipe out your enthusiasm.

There's a definite way to send the blues packing every time. Whenever a negative thought seems to try to dominate you, do your best to filter it out. This takes mental discipline at first, but if you continue allowing only good and positive thoughts to enter your mind, the blues will depart for other weaker minds.

6. Let money work for you. A growing savings account is money working for you. It may come in handy when you least expect it. When an opportunity presents itself, having a cash reserve can often mean the chance to take advantage of it.

Putting money to work can also mean investments. Not everyone has the extra funds to invest. If and when you do, with sound judgment, you might earn a handsome profit or even build a small to large fortune.

Big entertainment names and others all made a large part of their fortunes through wise and fortunate investments. Your money has little chance of growing if it's hoarded. It takes money to make more money.

7. Be systematic. Have the time and place for everything.

One proven method for a better daily organization is to make a list each night of the things you must do the next day to keep advancing and moving towards your goals and the increased success you seek. Then simply do the things you have listed each day. When you make out your list, whether it's for the next day or week, strive to put the items down in order of their importance. This will help to assure that you get the priority items done first.

Barnum made it his business to always have time for reading, a must for true success. He learned of the sale of the New York museum while reading a newspaper. Opening it as his own American Museum was an important step in his career because it led to better things later. Countless ideas that have led many to eventual or increased success and fortune have come from the daily reading of magazines and newspapers and books. In today's era we would add the Internet and electronic sources of information.

8. Advertise your business. Barnum strongly believed in this rule and followed it regularly in his own life and work. If P.T. Barnum, expert showman and promoter that he was, believed in advertising in the 1870s, you can quickly see how vital it is today in building a business to new levels of success.

When Barnum realized that his own fame was a major factor in his success, he fully exploited his name in promoting his circus. He has been compared to Shakespeare for his advertising eloquence. The reported author of statements like "there's a sucker born every minute," Barnum drew a sharp line between innocent humbug and outright fraud.

9. Do not scatter your powers—stick to one kind of business only—until you succeed or experience shows you must abandon it.

Barnum strongly believed that a fortune can slip through one's fingers when said person is working in too many occupations at a time. Still Barnum, a genius in his own right, defied his own warning, since he found time to run for Congress, to write his autobiography, to serve Bridgeport, Connecticut as mayor, and to open his own "Greatest Show on Earth" in Brooklyn.

There you have them, the guidelines and principles for increased success, the action steps of P.T. Barnum, perhaps the greatest showman and promoter of them all.

Barnum practiced what he thought daily and was widely known and loved for his sunny, alive nature, his constant desire to make people happy, and the improvement he brought to every town in which he lived. Reported to be worth five million when he died, he was also a very rich man in friends, family, and a sense of worthwhile achievement. His life and career brought happiness and entertainment to millions of people.

Barnum's principles for more success are certainly valid and on target for today's modern era. His principles and philosophy are well worth following today whatever your work is or your present and future dreams may be. Make Barnum's code for increased success a reality in your own work and life and then watch what happens. You'll be glad you followed his recipe and magic steps for higher vistas of success.

PART
V

PRACTICAL CONSIDERATIONS
FOR SPEAKERS

17

SET UP A SPEAKER'S RESOURCE GUIDE

One of the most helpful steps you could take to enhance and develop your skill for speaking in public is to set up a resource guide for future reference. Then whenever you speak to any group, even if it is only a short talk, referring to your resource guide would save you time and immediately help with your planning.

Today's new focus is on skilled communicators. Anything that can help you become a stronger speaker is well worth your time and attention.

What would go in your Speaker's Resource Guide (or file) would be anything and everything that you deem useful in your future speaking. This might include new ideas for talks and speeches, memorable examples that you could collect and then be able to look over, outline suggestions for new speeches, other supporting materials that you might wish to save, powerful openings to get attention in your introduction, effective anecdotes, research suggestions, ideas you get from the Internet, and more.

A TIME TESTED WAY TO IMPROVE

There is a tried and proven way in which you can improve

your skills as a communicator. Based on my past and present college level teaching experience in public speaking, I assure you that this method works. It has helped most of my students along with some adult classes I have taught. It has also helped my military students.

Both students and adults from all walks of life can use this method with good results. Some of my students even realized, through this method, that the communication field was the right vocation, the right place, for them.

Here is a summary of my proven method to make you a stronger communicator. It consists of two basic steps:

1. Buy yourself a fairly thick notebook or record book. Start at once to write down, or list, what *you* feel are good examples of communication. In other words, as you go about your daily routine and wherever you are on weekends, start collecting any and all examples of what you believe amounts to good or bad communication.

2. The second step is to consult your growing list frequently and think about what you have written down as good or bad communication.

After a few weeks or months, your list of communication examples will have grown considerably. The items you list can come from anywhere. Such examples might well cover many of the following:

1. Radio-television commercials you feel represent good or bad communication.
2. Magazine articles
3. Communications via the Internet
4. Other electronic materials
5. Newspaper editorials

6. Cartoons (yes, they communicate too)
7. Feature stories in newspapers or Sunday supplements
8. A billboard message
9. Humor in its many forms and variety
10. The key idea in a speech or address you heard or read
11. Print advertisements from some publication
12. Greeting cards because they communicate well and use a minimum number of words to do it.
13. Ideas from novels or nonfiction books
14. Items in newsletters or company publications
15. Comedy routine ideas
16. Various other sources

When you start collecting and keeping your list, be sure to write down the reason why you selected each example. Just tell briefly in your own words why you feel that each item is an example of good or bad communication. your comments might range from something like "good use of emotional appeal" to "reveals how the artful use of humor can cut through ice."

By recording the reasons you selected each example of communication, you can easily review your list at a later time, and you will be reminded why you chose each item. One of the examples in your list, for example, might look something like this:

5. Coffee commercial on television network show—It was poor communication because, as a whole, it seemed to insult the viewer's intelligence.

You can of course say more than the above example if you wish. But the basic idea is to cite your example of communication from whatever source and then tell why you feel it was a good, bad, or mediocre example.

Believe me, this works! If you start and maintain such a list for preferably three, six months, or longer, you are bound to learn more about communication. Why? Simply because you are observing and noting what you feel are good and bad examples from all the messages being beamed at you. You will thus become more sensitive in time to what strikes you as good quality or poor quality communication. You will be much more conscious of the wide varieties of possible examples, too.

Becoming a more skilled and effective communicator involves more than keeping a list of examples. Such a list helps to make you more aware of the material and ideas being directed at you every day. Read over your list frequently, at least once or twice a week, along with the reasons you put down for choosing each example.

This second step includes some of the basic things you can do to actually improve your speaking and communication ability. Some of these ideas will interest or appeal to you more than others. You probably will think of techniques you might want to try. Here are some action pointers that have helped many others. To improve as a speaker, you can do the following:

1. Listen to recordings of some of the world's finest speakers and voices. There is much inspiration to be gained in this way.

2. Attend lectures and addresses by the many speakers who visit your city, town, or surrounding regional area. Take a notebook with you and criticize them on paper. As you listen to them speak, try to determine how they could have done better.

3. Read some of the great speeches by famous speakers like Lincoln, Churchill, Daniel Webster, Bryan, Woodrow Wilson, and so on. This will get you familiar with the great orators of the past. You should

also listen to the strong speakers of today, the present day orators.

4. Practice speaking with a tape-recorder. Even thirty minutes or an hour a day can work wonders in your overall speaking ability. It will also greatly increase your confidence. Take notes when you play the tape back and then work to improve.

5. Sign up for a course in Speech Communication (often called Basic Speech, Public Speaking, or Fundamentals of Communication) at the nearest college or university in your area.

6. Offer to speak anywhere and everywhere for free. When you feel that you have gained enough confidence and have improved your speaking, you can then think about charging a fair fee to present your speaking program. Keep in mind that many places where you can speak will expect you to do it free. The idea here is to get started by speaking free. You are gaining skill, confidence, and learning each time you do this.

7. Consider offering to teach any kind of class for youth or adults. A skill you may have or previous back-ground-training might qualify you to teach a class. This front line teaching will require you to speak and communicate more every day.

Just thinking about upgrading your speaking ability, and then following through on some of the above suggestions, should enable you to add ideas of your own that seem especially right for you.

Collecting good quotes for talks and speeches will help you to stay alert. The same goes for collecting other materials and bits of information for future speeches. Quotes from leading individuals, or just interesting people in your community, can trigger ideas for interesting talks and speeches.

By speaking on a regular basis in your regional area, you will also discover that your skills are increasing. When this begins to happen, you may find that you truly enjoy standing in front of an audience and trying to inform, inspire, entertain, or persuade them.

What sharpens your ability is recording your reactions to talks and speeches you hear. What did you like and dislike? Where did the speakers fail to communicate and why? Did they grab and hold attention? Was the content worthy of the audience's time and attention? How did they do on posture, gestures, supporting materials, eye contact, and other areas? you always learn by evaluating speakers you hear.

Remember, if you really want to develop skill and power as a speaker, and possibly go places with it, you can certainly do so. It will take some time and effort, but you will definitely see the results if you stay with it. Try the notebook method, the saving or collection of good and bad examples of communication, and you will grow into a much stronger speaker.

18 _____

HOW TO LAUNCH YOURSELF
AS A PAID SPEAKER

The speaking-in-public route, sometimes called the lucrative lecture circuit, has become one of the great small businesses. Speaking for money has the potential of growing into a very profitable, full-time pursuit. You may well be able to build a second income as a part-time speaker.

Naturally, VIP names command the largest fees for speaking engagements. Speakers like Napoleon Hill, John Glenn, members of congress, film stars, celebrities, and well-known names receive large sums for their spoken dates.

Still unknowns are also earning thousands of dollars and more each year for speaking dates. Once you get started, lecturing can be an excellent way to increase your income and overall success.

FRINGE BENEFITS
In addition to the money, which can grow to be quite good as you gain speaking experience, the following fringe benefits are well worth the time and effort:

1. You make excellent contacts in a variety of national, possibly international, professional, business and historic organizations.

2. After you have spoken enough times and built a reputation, you may be in demand for all kinds of local seminars, business meetings, panel discussions, and a variety of solo speaking engagements for set fees.

3. your speaking sideline adds considerable prestige to your name and main line of work.

4. Speaking for money fits in nicely with your main business. You can, for example, speak locally or around the country on weekends.

5. You gain creative stimulation and pleasure from developing new topics and material for the programs you present before audiences.

6. You get to travel to interesting cities and sections of the country (possibly overseas, eventually). Speakers with a track record usually have all their expenses paid in getting to and from their speaking dates.

7. You develop into a four-star speaker with time and enough experience. Public speaking skill is a highly valuable quality to have. It can lead you almost anywhere.

HOW TO GET STARTED

The following tested directions will get you started in the speaking (lecture) business. You can follow these guidelines for part-time experience in the field. Along with the confidence you will gain as a speaker, you can soon begin to charge a fee for the programs you offer.

Try the speaking business on a part-time basis first and see if you like it and how well you do. You could speak only on weekends or several nights per month or quarter, or whatever will fit in with your main line of work.

Follow These Directions:

1. Make a list of lecture topics that interest you (those you think you would enjoy speaking on). Make careful notes of any special knowledge, information, or experience you have that might be developed into lecture programs. Material you already have will save you time and research. Again, choose subjects of interest to you and those you believe would make effective programs.

2. Narrow your lecture choices to one or two subjects (if you develop a lecture program from scratch). Then pick the one subject you like best and start researching. Decide how long you plan to speak. A twenty minute, or half-hour program, is a good length at first.

3. Gather material for your lecture from a variety of sources (including libraries, magazines, newspapers, books, booklets, newsletters, personal interviews you're able to line up with authorities, from seminars, business conferences, conventions, university classes, and so on).

4. Outline your lecture when you feel you have enough material. Here are some specific steps to help you:
a) Decide on the purpose of your lecture. Do you want

to inform, inspire, entertain, or persuade your
audience? The material for your lecture will vary
according to your purpose.
b) Zero in on the main parts to be covered in your
lecture. Simply decide what your main points will
consist of and in what order you will present them.
c) Strive to put the whole gist of your lecture into one
short sentence. This will help you throughout the
planning.
d) Arrange the main points or sections of your lecture in
what you believe will be the most effective order for
your audiences to hear. This may take some practice
and experimentation before it becomes clear which
points should go where.
e) Plan the supporting material you will use to back up
each of your main points. Your supporting material
will be more important when your purpose is to
persuade an audience.
f) Have a goal or objective to keep moving toward in
your lecture program.
g) Use specific images whenever possible. Audiences
think in pictures.
h) Be sure you have a strong attention-getting opening, a
good middle part, and satisfying ending for your
lecture.

5. Write your speech striving to make it as strong as
possible. Tape-record some of it and pretend you are
sitting in the audience.
    Rewrite any vague or confusing points or sections.
Always keep in mind that the material of your lecture
will be orally presented before a live audience.

6. Start practicing your lecture out loud just the way you
intend to present it before an audience. You must learn

it so well that you will not have to lose eye contact with your audience (or at least very seldom). You can use notes on index cards while presenting your lecture, or you can refer to an outline of your material. Learn your lecture or program so well that you can be ready to emphasize certain points with gestures. The communication quality of your lecture or program will be far better if you do not have to look at notes, an outline, or anywhere but right at your audience. Speakers, for example, who read their material in front of an audience do not really have the right to consider themselves speakers. In truth they are readers.

Again, recording or video-taping your lecture can be a great help. Listen to it carefully, making notes on how you can improve your presentation. Have a friend or family member listen to you and offer suggestions for or improvement. Spoken programs and lectures are perfected through practice and more practice.

7. Design a brochure. This is not difficult, and it should include highlights of your background. If possible, a small picture should appear in the brochure plus the title of your lecture program (or programs if you have more than one).

Use a good small picture of yourself, taken perhaps while speaking. Be sure your name, address, and telephone number are on your brochure.

8. Have at least several thousand copies of your brochure printed (once you have what you believe is a professional looking one). Or you could just have a few hundred printed to see if it will bring in any speaking dates for you.

9. The next step is to start selling yourself as a speaker. Send your brochure on the program (or programs) you offer to associations, schools, women's clubs, and to any organization using speakers for its yearly or semi-annual or monthly meetings. Try to find the names of program chairmen and chair women because they are the ones who choose speakers. Send your brochure to them and also try to contact them in person whenever possible.

10. As a new speaker, you will probably find it difficult to line up your first speaking engagement. Be prepared to speak free in the beginning. After all, you need the experience. If and when you do speak free, wherever it is, always request a written letter commending you for the program you presented (assuming all went well and the audience was pleased).

Then save those letters for they can be used to get new speaking dates. Such letters sell you to other groups that use speakers, for they reason that if one club or organization was pleased with you as a speaker, they might well be too.

It's also smart to take your brochure to schools in person. By schools I mean high schools, colleges, and special types of schools; you could ask for a small fee (at first) plus the going rate for gas mileage if you drive to and from the place you speak.

When you go by schools in person, with your brochure, express your interest in speaking to a student group. This often works well and particularly so if you have a lecture program suitable or of special interest to young people.

In other words, sell yourself as a speaker in person whenever possible because you will usually get more speaking engagements this way. Use the mail of course, too, sending out your brochures and asking for a speaking engagement. Try to be as businesslike as possible, whether dealing with those individuals responsible for choosing speakers (in person) or via the mail.

In time you should be able to start charging a small fee, at least, each time you speak. With increasing experience and speaker credits (places where you have spoken previously), you can raise your fee to whatever you think the traffic will bear.

There are speaker (lecture) agencies that represent professional speakers. Their job is to obtain engagements for you, and they take a percentage of your fee for their service.

Most speaker agencies will not consider handling you until you have more or less proved that you can do well in front of a variety of audiences. It's possible, however, to persuade an agent to take you on at an earlier point in time. Some speakers achieve this by offering to speak free as a kind of test audition. They then so impress the audience and agency that they are taken on as regular speaker-client by an established agency.

Most new speakers, however, will have to go it alone until they begin to develop a name and contacts in the field who will ask for them as speakers again and again and suggest that other clubs and groups use them as speakers.

When it all begins to jell for you as a speaker, that is when you may find that you are increasing in demand. The bottom line of all this is simply that the time needed to go places as a speaker varies and depends on a number of factors. Keep this in mind at the beginning when you may experience difficulties in lining up speaking engagements.

MAKE A START
Think of speaking as a worthy part-time activity. Make a start and do your best to become a professional speaker (a paid

one) and see what happens. Even if you do just fairly well, you will add income and valuable contacts plus gain that very important confidence and experience on the platform (the pro speaker's platform). Who knows? It might turn out to be a very successful sideline route for you, which could perhaps lead eventually to a highly rewarding, full-time future for you on the lucrative lecture circuit.

Each annual edition of *Literary Market Place* (LMP) lists lecture agencies that represent professional speakers. These addresses change, so check each new edition and you will have the names of some of the best known speaker agents. Most large libraries have LMP, so you would not have to purchase a copy but can refer to the agencies via a simple visit to your library.

Remember, each professional speaker now doing well on the lecture program circuit was once a beginner. Developing a great looking brochure that offers several interesting program topics can be a most important step. You must have such a brochure, and plenty of copies of it, to promote yourself as a speaker. Once you get going and are picking up fees for your programs, you should find it easier to interest an agency in representing you.

If professional speaking is what you want, be determined. Practice your lecture programs, work up some strong subjects that will grab interest. Then sell yourself via your brochure and in person whenever possible. There is real power in a determined person, a strong speaker who knows where he or she is going and how to get there.

Refer to this chapter for guidance and inspiration, for it is based on proven steps that have worked well for many others including some on the rewarding lecture circuit today. Good luck and many paid speaking engagements to you.

19

QUESTIONS AND ANSWERS FOR FUTURE REFERENCE

Here are some of the most frequently asked questions regarding the art of speaking in public and the answers. These questions and answers are meant to encourage you in your own speaking. Refer to this chapter as you grow and develop into a more powerful speaker:

Q: What is the very best way to introduce a speech?

A: Opinions vary on this. Some believe that a reference to the occasion for the speech is good. Others say the use of an example leading into the subject is very effective. Still other views include paying the audience a compliment, stressing the importance of the subject, or identifying with the audience in some way.

I think it's helpful to experiment with different types of introductions. In this way, you will sooner or later find the best introduction for a given speech you plan to present. Sometimes just a direct opening statement works well.

A strong quote, anecdote, or powerful example that gets to the heart of your topic can work too. Many gripping and compelling speeches have opened with a startling statement of some kind, a series of questions, or a memorable story.

Q: What should a speaker do when he or she forgets what comes next?

A: First, try to stay in control of the situation. Do not panic. A long pause can give you a chance to recover and get back on the track of your speech.

If you know the ideas and content of your speech or talk well enough, you could paraphrase the material; say it in a different way but still your own. If you know the thoughts behind the words, it's always possible to transmit the material in a variety of ways.

Another option is to summarize what you have already said. While doing this, you can decide in your mind how to proceed from that point.

Q: What is "audience feedback?"

A: The reactions of an audience let a speaker know what kind of communication is taking place. If some listeners in the audience, for example, appear to be straining to hear, it may mean that you are not speaking loud enough. Other signs from the audience are puzzled looks, listeners who look away, frowns, and nods of agreement. This is why eye contact is so very important.

Q: What are the major benefits of a college course in public speaking?

A: The most valuable benefit is the experience you will gain from speaking before the rest of the class. The more speeches and presentations you are required to give in a course, the better it will prove to be. Other helpful benefits are learning how to choose a suitable subject, discovering the skills of presenting a speech, planning, outlining, and writing a speech, and finding out about the various branches of speech communication.

Q: Does reading a speech out loud help to learn the material when preparing?

A: I certainly think so. It helps to establish the pattern of ideas and thoughts in your mind. Along with reading the material out loud, it's also a great help to tape-record the speech and listen to it a number of times.

Q: Which type of speech is the hardest to present?

A: This is a matter of opinion. Many believe that the speech to entertain is the hardest, because it can be difficult to amuse an audience. In my own opinion, I believe the speech to persuade often proves to be the hardest. This is especially true if the views, ideas, and beliefs of the audience are stubbornly held and, therefore hard to change or influence.

Q: Does the study of public speaking help in choosing the right job or vocation?

A: Very much. I majored in Speech Communication in college, and it was during this time that I realized I wanted to spend my life in some branch of communications.

My study of speech pointed me in the right direction. It propelled me into the right arena. It has done the same for many others. In a class on beginning debate, which I helped teach at Murray State University, two college seniors found themselves. They became enormously interested in debate and took part in the entire debate competition, including tournaments, for the year. They won some major debates with students from other universities. Near the end of the term these two graduating seniors told the rest of us that they were going on to law school and that the debate course (a branch or area of speech communication) had made them realize that was what they wished to do.

Q: What is the best thing to do when and if some listeners in an audience continue to talk and whisper while a speech is being presented?

A: A long pause often works well, while looking intently at the two who are talking. Sometimes a dramatic or surprising (even startling) statement will work, providing your material includes it.

Humor is often the best way out of any awkward situation. If you can come up with a great one-liner or statement that brings out some humor, that can often solve any problem.

Q: What pleases an audience most in a speaker and subject matter?

A: Audiences will vary of course, but generally speaking most of them want to hear something they can talk about later to their friends or family members. New information pleases them because it lets them come away with the feeling that they have learned something.

Funny or interesting stories are popular, and the same goes for provocative ideas. Actually there are many things that can please an audience. If you communicate your own strong interest and excitement about your material, your audience will tend to feel that their time was well spent listening to your speech.

Q: What is meant by the integrity of a speaker?

A: As a speaker you are expected to do the necessary advance preparation for presenting an effective talk or speech. Audiences have the right to expect professional material or at least speeches that are worthwhile and presented as well as possible.

Q: Is the subject of a speech more important than the person who presents it?

A: No. I would say that the speaker is just as important. One may have a marvelous subject for a speech or talk, but if the material is not effectively presented, much of the potential subject value will be lost. The reason is that if the material cannot be communicated well, most of the audience will tune out the speaker.

Q: I can't decide between two different topics for a speech. What should I do?

A: Think about the way you would handle each subject. Which topic do you feel you could handle most effectively? Then, too, one of the subjects may be better suited for your audience.

Consider also the occasion of the speech, if any, and some of the facts about your audience (education level, general age, their interest in the subject). In other words, examine each subject in view of your audience. Thinking about your audience and the way you would handle each subject will help you reach the right decision.

Q: What advice can you offer for a speaker who often has trouble deciding how to end a talk?

A: Try to find the best way to tie-it-all-together. Sometimes a strong example or quotation will do it. Seek to bring your presentation to a logical and satisfying ending. As a strong example, here is how Winston Churchill concluded an action speech by using the rhetoric or repetition, a poetic device:

> We shall not flag nor fail. We shall go on to the end, we shall fight in France, we shall fight on the seas and oceans, we shall fight with growing confidence and strength in the air, we shall defend our island, whatever the cost may be, we shall fight on the beaches, we shall fight on the landing grounds, we shall fight in the fields and in the streets, we shall fight in the hills, we shall never surrender.

Q: What is impromptu speaking?

A: It shows a speaker the difficulty of speaking without preparation. Impromptu speaking is getting up and sounding forth on a given subject with no time to prepare at all. It's spur-of-the moment speaking often thought of and called "thinking on your feet." It can be a useful exercise in learning how to evaluate the vocal and communication habits of a speaker.

Q: Gestures worry me when I speak. Can you tell me what to do with my hands:

A: Rather than use the same gestures, try instead for a variety. Generally speaking, use small gestures when speaking to a small audience and wide or big ones when addressing a large crowd. If most of the members of your audience are on the young side, use a plentiful number of gestures. A younger audience usually likes to see more gestures, although there is no binding rule on it.

The normal place for your arms and hands, when not gesturing, is at your sides or on the sides of the podium.

Q: How much money do professional speakers make?

A: It depends on how many times they speak each year and the size of the fees they receive. Some well-known speakers get $10,000, $20,000 and more for a single engagement. A big film name or celebrity reportedly receives $30,000 and $40,000 for a speaking program. The size of the fee you can charge depends on how much experience you have, who the speaking is done for (national association, local club, civic group, or whatever), how much in demand your topic or program is, how far you have to travel to keep the engagement, and whether you offer any special features in your program. Once you are in demand as a speaker, it can mean many thousands and up every time you speak.

Q: Certain speakers I hear at times are very hard to follow. Why is this so when others are most interesting?

A: Unfortunately, there are speakers who have not learned to say what they mean. They may not communicate or get across to an audience. It is also true that they may not have practiced enough (ahead of time) to be well prepared.

Q: What is the definition of an ideal orator?

A: Cicero, perhaps the greatest orator of all time, once gave his definition of the ideal orator: "In an orator, the acuteness of the logicians, the wisdom of the philosophers, the memory of lawyers, the voice of tragedians, the gesture almost of the best actors, is required. Nothing, therefore, is more rarely found among mankind than a consummate orator." I find it hard to improve on this definition of an orator.

Q: How can I best cope with this fear of speaking that I've always had?

A: Just be prepared as best you can. Know your material so well that you have confidence in it and yourself. Know also that you have worthwhile material that will help the audience in some way (inform, entertain, inspire, or persuade). Breathing deeply before speaking seems to help a lot of nervous speakers. As for the long run, I believe the best cure for the fear of speaking comes from experience behind a podium before an audience. The more speaking you do the less fear you will have in time.

Q: The last speaker I heard looked at his watch several times during the speech. Wasn't this the wrong thing to do?

A: When speaking you should not look at your watch—at least not in an obvious way. A small watch could be placed on the podium in a way that the speaker could easily glance at it and know the time if necessary. No watch is needed, however, if a speaker has practiced enough and knows the exact time of the speech or sections of it.

Some speakers do place a watch with a large dial on the lectern beside their notes for quick time checks. Just be careful you don't send the watch flying with a sweeping gesture you might make during your talk. Yes, it has happened before to some speakers.

Q: What is the purpose of the supporting materials of a speech?

A: They are used to back up the main points of a speech and are very important.

Q: What are some signs of a poor speaker?

A: Leaning on the podium or lectern, bobbing back and forth on the feet, moving from side to side too much, reading the speech, no gestures, too fast or slow a rate of speaking, and little or no voice variety or a dull and lifeless voice.

Q: What is meant by the ethics of the speaker?

A: Ethics means honest as a speaker and doing one's own work. It also includes being well-prepared and using suitable material. A speaker has a basic responsibility to not waste the time of an audience but to have worthwhile content and to communicate it well.

Q: Can the power of a speaker's personality make the content or a talk or speech sound and come across better than it really is?

A: Most definitely, but the goal to shoot for is strong content that is also presented in a dynamic way. Both what is said and how it's communicated are important.

Q: How can too fast a speaking rate be improved?

A: Practice can help a great deal and also the knowledge that there are ways to improve it. Working with a tape recorder can provide the speaker with immediate proof that efforts to slow down the pace are working. The speaker can listen back to the tape and determine if the effort to slow down is working. With effort and time plus the conscious focus of slowing the pace whenever you speak, much improvement can be realized.

Q: What is articulation in the speech process?

A: It means the clear pronunciation of words and syllables.

Q: Would the topic of "Overseas Transportation" be a good one for a speech?
A: No, because it is too broad. It needs to be narrowed to something you can handle, a segment of what you now have. Trying to speak on overseas transportation would be like trying to swim the Atlantic Ocean. Every speech topic should be narrowed enough to a central idea about that subject. Try to zero in on the subject like a camera and look for an angle on the subject, a segment that you can deal with effectively.

Q: Can a blackboard or chalkboard be used when presenting a speech?
A: Yes, if it is used in a limited way. The trouble with using a board is that some speakers spend too much time writing or drawing on the board, and this means their backs are to the audience for too long a time. The board is fine to use to highlight certain points. Just be certain you use it in a limited way.

Q: What is the difference between conversation and speaking in public?
A: Conversation is informal, but a speech is much more elaborate and well-planned. Conversation is spur-of-the-moment communication in most cases, while a speech is a formal presentation before an audience.

Q: Would a speech or talk titled "Kids Say the Funniest Things" be a potentially good speech to entertain?
A: Yes, it is narrow enough to work, offers promise, and could be an effective speech.

Q: Can you suggest some good ways to end or conclude a speech?
A: Your main objective is to bring the speech or talk in for

a "happy landing." You do not want to end too abruptly and thus leave the audience hanging on a cliff top so to speak. Some proven, time-tested ways to end a speech include the use of a quote that ties it all together, an anecdote or little story that wraps it all up, and these other methods:

- Summarize the speech (most speeches end with a summary.)
- Look to the future.
- Repeat the most important main point of your talk.
- Challenge your audience in some way regarding the subject.
- Call your audience to action regarding the topic.

There are still others ways to end a speech, but the above are some of the most often used methods. Most talks and speeches probably use a summary to conclude.

Q: Has a speaker failed if the audience does not laugh a lot in the speech to entertain?
A: No. The main objective or goal in this speech is to amuse the audience. Audiences can be amused without howling with laughter all the way through a talk or speech. It's okay if they laugh some, and humor is good for this speech, but no speaker should feel failure if the audience does not laugh. If you as a speaker have amused the audience, then you have succeeded.

Q: Should a talk or speech be completely written out first?
A: If you intend to have the manuscript in front of you, then the answer is yes. I think it's best to experiment with all the key ways to present a speech including full manuscript (providing you don't end up reading it all), memory, using outline-notes, and the extemporaneous method, in which you use only key phrases or lines on index cards. This last method, the extemporaneous way of speaking, is the one used by most professionals.

Q: Can you give an example of using the note method?

A: It can be an elaborate outline or simply a list of steps for the speaker to use. Here are the notes I used for a short speech. You will notice that the notes are simply phrases or short sentences:

1. Give the Edgar Allan Poe quotation.
2. Emphasize the four major causes of failure.
3. Open a question-and-answer period at this point.
4. Summarize guidelines for living.
5. Florida illustration comes next.

If you are speaking on a long and involved subject, a brief and simple outline or notes won't work. In such a case, you might want a more solid outline.

Keep in mind that the type of outline you learned to do in school may be used for many talks and speeches. This outline is formed with a large letter, a number, a small letter combination. Various versions of the letter and number combination are used, depending upon the need of the speaker or the way the person wishes to do the outline. Only part of the outline is given:

A. Introduce speech with a startling, or shocking, story illustration of how fear cripples a human being.

    1. Cite several relevant quotes from experts on fear.

B. First main point—There is a rogues gallery of all kinds of fear.

    1. Example of millions of Americans who are afraid to go out at night in large cities.

Q: If a speaker has a good memory, why not memorize the talk or speech?

A: When you use this method, and some persons can do well via this method (though they are few), you go to the podium armed with nothing but your memory. It better be reliable and trustworthy, or you will find yourself in trouble fast.

The human mind can go blank at any time. Say a fire engine or ambulance goes by, or an airplane goes right over the place you are speaking, and wham, your memory is suddenly blank. It does happen.

If your talk or speech is short, and you trust your memory enough, then by all means try this method. Some few persons do have sharp memories, and speaking this way enables you to eliminate any use of notes, outline, index cards, or full manuscript. Again, it's probably best to test your memory and experiment with how you speak from memory alone.

Q: Are personal interviews helpful in obtaining material for a talk or speech?

A: Yes, they can be strong supporting materials for some of your main points. Personal interview information and material let the audience know that it's not just you, the speaker, claiming or stating these points. Such interviews serve as evidence and support for the main points of a talk.

Q: Can a speech to inform also have elements of inspiration, entertainment, and persuasion?

A: Yes. Its main purpose is to inform, but it can cross borders and also include material that inspires, entertains, or persuades the audience. Many fine speeches cross borders, even though their main purpose is clear.

Q: Could you name some of the visual aid choices that a speaker might use?

A: There are many of them and include the use of a blackboard the use of posters, drawings, handouts to the audience, slides, pictures, charts, maps, designs, and others.

Appendix I _____

A SELF-SCORING TEST
ON SPEAKING

Your answers to the following test questions will help you to determine which areas to work on to improve your speaking skills. Answer the questions with either a "yes" or "no" and then refer to the directions for scoring your test:

1. Do you feel there is room for improvement in general as a speaker and communicator?

2. Are you willing to work on some weekends and weeknights, too, in order to advance as a speaker?

3. Do you think you would enjoy speaking to audiences more, if you could gain more experience at it?

4. Do you like to listen to well-known speakers who visit in your area?

5. Do you accept any invitations to speak to various groups in your surrounding area?

6. When you achieve one of your goals, do you start moving forward toward the next one on your list?

7. Do you agree that the ability to speak well could add power and more success to your life?

8. Can you think of several subjects that interest you as possible ideas for speeches?

9. Are you presently using all or most of your abilities and resources to get ahead?

10. Does the idea of speaking before a group of people interest you?

11. Do people sometimes tell you that you have a pleasant voice or that you would make a good speaker?

12. If it meant advancement and a higher income, would you be willing to travel around the country (and maybe overseas), in order to speak to various audiences and groups?

13. Are you sometimes inspired by a local, regional, or nationally prominent speaker?

14. Do you find yourself talking with your hands, when describing or narrating something to a friend?

15. Do you think it would be challenging or interesting to practice a speech presentation by using a tape-recorder?

16. Do you feel it would be fun to be an after-dinner

speaker, with the ability to amuse and entertain audiences?

17. Do you believe it would be worth the time and effort to develop a lecture program for presentation before a variety of audiences?

18. Does the idea or prospect of becoming a successful speaker on the profitable lecture circuit excite you?

19. Have you ever attended an all-day seminar of speeches by speakers who are authorities on certain subjects (say investments, for example)? These seminars are frequently offered in many major cities.

20. Do you think you might have something to contribute as a part-time speaker (and possibly a full-time speaker at some point in the future)?

HOW TO SCORE YOUR TEST ANSWERS

Score five points for every yes answer and zero for each no answer. Then add your total to get your score.

Evaluation of Your Score

Score 90-100

Excellent! Your high score shows you have a strong interest in public speaking. You could go far in the field, possibly, with this fine potential. You should think about becoming a professional speaker.

Score 80-90

This is a good level of potential. It may be that you should consider getting into public speaking, or some form of communications, as a part-time sideline. The seeds of success are there.

Score 70-80

You have a fair degree of interest in the speaking/communication field. While you are somewhat limited in what you might achieve, you might be able to develop from this point.

Score Under 70

Based on this score, you do not have enough interest or motivation.

Appendix II _____

WHEN IT'S TIME TO GIVE YOUR SPEECH

Since red-letter days come for most of us, sooner or later you may have to present a speech before a live audience. Instead of letting panic set in as your speech date looms ever closer, you can be cool, calm, and collected by being prepared to stand up and speak up with confidence.

The ability to speak well is power, but even if you've never spoken before an audience, or despite a time lapse of years since your last speech, you can hold your own and do well at the podium, provided you've done some advance thinking and planning. Being ready is the key to your public speaking success.

It's important to understand that some fear of speaking in public is natural. A great many people have this fear, so there's no reason to be ashamed of it. In fact, most speakers do better because of at least a small amount of nervousness. Reasons for too great a fear of speaking include the fear of making a mistake and looking like a fool, the fear of getting up in front of strangers, and the fear of your mind going blank—of forgetting what comes next in your speech.

I taught public speaking on the university level for a number of years, and I'm here to tell you that the greatest obstacle between a speaker and his or her audience is this business of fear.

This old bugaboo, fear, can paralyze the vocal cords, tie up throat muscles, and give a speaker the quickest case of lockjaw you've ever seen. In the beginning of each speech class I led, my single most important goal was to help my students to rise above this fear of standing in front of other people and speaking to them. The best way to overcome this fear is to practice. In the privacy of your home, apartment, or office, actually go through your speech just like you intend to give it before an audience. Enough practice will develop a great deal of confidence.

Many skilled speakers tape-record their speeches and then listen to the tape, taking notes on how they can improve their effectiveness. Others ask a friend, relative, or family member to hear part, or all, of their speeches and then offer suggestions on how the speech might be improved. However, bear in mind that some speakers take criticism of their presentations better than others.

It can help to keep in mind that a speech is simply the communication of thoughts and ideas through the use of words, gestures, eye contact, voice quality and variety, plus the overall personality of the speaker. Some speakers can say a lot in a relatively short speech. Others say little in a long speech.

Becoming a better communicator is well worth the effort. In the words of Clarence Randall, the former Chairman of the Board of Inland Steel Corporation, "We are cut off from the public because we can neither write nor speak the English language with clarity and force." If one can learn to be a stronger communicator, his or her business or professional career is bound to be more successful.

The four basic types of speeches include the speech to inform, the speech to persuade or convince, the speech to entertain, and the speech to inspire. The purpose of these speeches sometimes overlap, because a speech to inform, for example, may also persuade, entertain, and inspire.

The speech to inform is one of the most important kinds of speeches. Some examples of this type of speech are: "How to

Get More Out of Your Leisure Time," "The Shrinking Value of College Degree," and "Coping With the Battle of the Bulge." Each of these possible speeches might well persuade, entertain, or inspire, in addition to informing.

Aristotle, who wrote a master work on the art of persuasion and rhetoric, said that "the use of a persuasive speech is to lead to decisions."

In order for it to persuade an audience, a speech must make strong use of such tools as evidence; the testimony, opinions, views, and statements of known authorities; clear and specific examples; comparisons; and the presentation of all persuasive ideas (of the speech) in a meaningful way.

The belief and conviction of some members of an audience are rather easy to change by a skilled speaker, but others in every audience may be much more difficult to sway. To persuade those holding mildly held beliefs, you simply need to have a solid number of logical and sound reasons why the listeners should change their opinions. When the beliefs held are very strong, however, you will need all the persuasive power you can bring to bear on the matter. This means evidence, and lots of it. This evidence should be in the form of facts, statements and quotes by noted experts in the field, illustrations, statistics, and all the supporting ammunition you can muster. The majority of persuasive speeches are meant to stimulate attitudes of listeners.

When planning your speech to persuade, it's wise to decide exactly what you seek to persuade your audience about. Then determine in advance how you intend to go about accomplishing this goal. Ask yourself how the audience can be persuaded. This type of speech takes careful planning and outlining.

You must try to get the audience to not only accept you, as a speaker, but also to believe what you say. A few examples of this type of speech are "Teaching Deserves Your Best" (presented to an audience of teachers), and "The Case for Talking Things Out" (to persuade the audience of the value and benefits of discussing issues and problems, instead of remaining silent).

Many consider a speech to entertain to be the most popular, and it may well be the favorite speech to listen to. To entertain is to bring pleasure to others. It's a worthy goal.

Another way of defining or thinking of this type of speech is to view it as an after-dinner speech. It has long been traditional to expect an after-dinner speaker to be an entertaining one, though this doesn't always turn out to be the case. When many groups of people gather to have dinner and then listen to a chosen speaker, people want the speaker to entertain them. Such speeches may also be informative in places, and even include elements of inspiration and persuasion, but the overall purpose is to entertain the audience.

If this is the kind of speech you wish to present, you need to focus on a subject that is attractive, amusing, something light and sparkling, a topic with a strong degree of interest, and definitely a subject with entertainment appeal for the audience.

In a real sense, subjects which offer escape often work well. Through your choice of subject and presentation, it's entirely possible to take your listeners on a journey. Speakers who present programs on travel to exotic lands or glamorous cities are a good example of this escapism benefit. Their programs entertain audiences, while informing them at the same time.

Showmanship helps in this speech. Showmanship is not deceit or trickery; it means to brighten up something and make it attractive, enjoyable, and appealing. Many figures in the entertainment world have this ability. Watch them and try to pick up some of their techniques.

Here are some proven ways for creating an amusing effect in the speech to entertain. Open your speech with an unusual remark. Poke fun at yourself in some way. Another option is to relate an amusing story or anecdote. Perhaps you can refer to a humorous experience you've recently had.

This type of speech usually fares better with a brisk pace. Try to sound friendly and act like you're enjoying yourself. Make your audience feel like you're gland to be there speaking to them.

You'll need crisp and vivid illustrations and anecdotes for this kind of speech. Some likely sources for useful illustrations include your own recent amusing experience, other entertaining things that have happened to you, interesting material form the lives of others you know, and family adventures. You can also include something you hear on television or read in a magazine. There's a variety of sources for amusing material.

Don't use all your best material in the early part of your speech. Save some of the most amusing bits for the latter part and ending of the speech.

Another main reason or purpose for speaking to an audience is to inspire them. In this speech, an idea, viewpoint, subject, or theory is cast in such a light, or communicated in such an ennobled way (by you, the speaker) that the listener comes away with a fresh, vivid, and possibly exciting new perspective. The listener feels an influence to make his or her life count more. A change in the listener's basic attitude takes place.

To attempt to inspire an audience, speak from your heart. This kind of communication is powerful and can inspire. Believe so much in the subject and material of your speech that it will come across to your audience. Do your best to stir your listeners to the very core of their beings. In other words, move them by your speech in such a way that they will be different people form that point on. Above all, use the power of your personality to make your material inspiring. Make them remember you in the weeks and months to come, not just the ABC's of your speech material.

A good example of the speech to inspire is one I heard a few years ago titled "Nothing Can Defeat Man's Indomitable Spirit." I still remember this speech. It was most inspiring.

As you plan your speech, remember that a strong speech will have three essential parts. They are the introduction, middle part, and conclusion.

The introduction is the most important of the three, because without an attention-getting opening, you will lose most of your audience. The introduction hooks the attention of the audience, puts the spotlight on the subject, and tells the audience why they should listen.

Once you know the subject, central idea (the angle) of your speech, its purpose, and the overall response you seek from the audience, you are ready to plan and write your speech. Here is an example of the way a speech on the subject of money might evolve:

Subject—Money

Central idea (angle of the subject)—To tell the audience how to build a second income.

Purpose sentence—To inform the audience of the most practical ways to build a supplementary income.

Desired audience response—To teach the audience how to add to their yearly income, and to motivate them to put one or more plans into action.

Introduction—Use quotes and shocking statements on today's decreased spending value of the dollar—and on rising inflation. Explain the need for a side or extra income.

Middle part of speech—Present the main points on how a second income can be realized. Back up the main points with supporting materials, such as testimony, evidence, quotes by authorities and statistics.

Conclusion of speech—End with either a summary of the main points or an effective anecdote illustration on the value and importance of an extra source of money in today's modern era.

You can use the above outline example as a guide whenever you plan to speak to an audience. Remember that once you know your subject for a speech, do your best to sum up the thrust of the speech in one important purpose sentence. With a purpose sentence to refer back to while planning and writing your speech, you are much more likely to know where you want to go. Then check your speech, as it develops, to be sure it's continuing in the right direction.

There are four key ways to present a speech to an audience. Some would say five. The four ways include knowing the speech so well that you need nothing to remind yourself what to say, the use of notes, using only an outline, and speaking from memory. There's another method, which is the use of a full manuscript, but this isn't really an effective form of presentation. If you have your entire speech written down in front of you on the podium, you will probably tend to read it, and thus lose valuable eye contact with your audience.

Not using any tools at all is an excellent way to speak. Why? Because you're in constant contact with your audience. When you know your speech material so well that you simply stand up on your two feet, look them in the eye, and present your speech, you have the best chance to communicate effectively. This naturally means a lot of practice and going over your material many times until you have mastered it completely.

For insurance that your mind doesn't go blank, you can type or write a key line or phrase for each succeeding idea-point of your speech. Place these key phrases on index cards and place them on the podium. Then, in case you're not sure what comes next, you have only to glance at the next card. This method serves to trigger your mind on what comes next.

Speaking from memory alone can be quite tricky, and it's not recommended for most speakers. Some do claim success with this method, but such speakers usually have a terrific memory. Unless you have a superb memory, and feel you can trust it, I don't advise you to use this form of presentation.

It's a good idea to experiment with the basic ways of presenting a speech until you find the method you like best. When you practice your speech, strive for voice variety, the use of gestures, pauses after certain points or statements in your speech, and contrast in the pace and rhythm of your material as you present it. Recording a rehearsal of your speech can help you learn a great deal about your voice, delivery defects, strong points, and overall presentation.

I cannot overemphasize the importance of practice. The way to become an excellent speaker, and even have a chance to join the profitable professional speaker's circuit, is to practice each speech you give so much that you please the audiences you address and achieve a high degree of quality communication.

Above all, keep growing and building confidence and skill as a public speaker. It will enrich your life and the lives of all those in the audience. The speeches you present may well touch the lives of many people, especially if you give many speeches over a long period of time, and help these people to get more out of their lives in any number of ways. It's a wonderful feeling to know you're ready when it's time to give your speech. More power to you!

Index _____

HOW TO BE REALLY FUNNY

by Mark Stolzenberg

Humor is an important element in public speaking, but not all speakers are good humorists. A good speaker can tell a bad joke and make it funny. A bad speaker can tell a great joke—but have it fall flat simply because of the way it is told.

In this book, you will learn the secrets used by professional speakers and comedians to make people roar with laughter. Discover how to effectively use body language, facial expressions, comic gestures, your voice, and props to enhance your presentation.

Comedian Mark Stolzenberg has been electrifying audiences in just about every theatrical medium. He is a master speaker, showman, and entertainer. He has made numerous television appearances, acted in films and on stage, and has performed in nightclubs and cabarets, at elementary schools, high schools, colleges and universities. He is the author of three books on comedy technique and performance.

You can get a copy of this unique book from your local book dealer or send $16 (USA and Canada only) to Piccadilly Books, Ltd., P.O. Box 25203, Colorado Springs, CO 80936, USA. (For addresses outside USA and Canada please inquire.)

Write and ask for a free catalog of other unique and fun books published by Piccadilly Books, Ltd.